Jonathan Spurrell is a freelance translator and amateur historian. He has been researching his family history for almost twenty years and has written a number of articles for local history societies. His interests are in social, political and landscape history, particularly in Norfolk and East Anglia. This is his first book. He currently lives in the United States with his wife and two daughters.

D1288584

BESSINGHAM

The Story of a Norfolk Estate

1766 ~ 1970

Published 2016
by Jonathan Spurrell

Copyright © Jonathan Spurrell

www.bessinghamhistory.org

ISBN 978-1-5262-0597-1

Printed by Barnwell Print Ltd.
Aylsham, Norfolk, NR11 6SU
Tel.: 01263 732767

To the memory of my late grandfather

Charles Frederick Stuart Spurrell
(1904-1981)

CONTENTS

ACKNOWLEDGEMENTS

I am indebted to all the people who have shown an interest in this project and taken the time to write or speak to me about life in Bessingham now and in the past. I am grateful to Alfred Blake, Nell Burling (née Hudson), George Finch, Ted Finch, Patricia Hill, Jez Hull, Joyce Knowles (née Mallett), Roy Lawrence, Nicholas Lyle, Rosie Purdy (née Wiseman), Roy Street, David Swainston, Gill Webb (née Hudson), Joy White (née Wright) and Bill Wright for sharing memories and information with me. I am grateful to Bob Gamble for speaking candidly with me in 2008 about his time in Bessingham; to Tim Schofield for allowing me to see the Manor House in 2010 when its restoration looked far from certain; to William and Dawn Hickey for giving me tours of the house both during and after its restoration; to Michael Day and John Shelly for their hospitality and for keeping me informed of developments in the village; to Peter Wrighton for sharing his photograph collection and giving me a tour of the farmhouse and outbuildings at Manor House Farm; to Jackie and Alan Almond for allowing me to attend the village party at Rectory Cottage in 2013; to Ian Clarke for letting me explore the former parkland and the ruins of the old manor house; to Cane Rounce for providing me with documents to photograph; to Mary Willcox (née Ives) for sharing her memories of Denham Spurrell, and to her son Simon for allowing me to study family photographs and quote from his great-grandmother's journal; to Sheridan Hughes for answering my many questions about his grandfather, Ronald Hitchcock; to John and Judy McNeil Wilson for passing on information about the daffodil breeder Katherine Spurrell and for letting me see their beautiful garden; to Sharon McDonald, formerly the International Daffodil Registrar at the Royal Horticultural Society, for her interest in the work of Katherine Spurrell; to Priscilla and Henry Macdougall for discussing the history of Sustead Old Hall and for their kindness when showing me around and on other occasions; to John and Mags Neill for chatting about farming and village life in Bessingham and Thurgarton over generous glasses of whisky; to Christopher Pipe for his helpful advice and for seeking out locations in Aylmerton and Cromer for me; to Richard May for sharing his unrivalled knowledge of the history of Sidestrand; to Tim Mills for allowing me to photograph the scrapbook that belonged to his grandfather, the Rev. W. W. Mills, and for giving me several letters, photographs and other items that belonged to Daniel Spurrell and his family; and to Diana Hayward for sharing her memories of the Mills sisters of Roughton and giving me a box of paintings and photographs that once belonged to them.

I would like to thank Shelagh Hutson for discussing her family's connections with Bessingham over a delightful lunch at County Hall in 2013 and for accepting my invitation to write the foreword to this book. I am grateful also to the late John Shrive for inviting me to his office in Holt to discuss his role in the sale of the Bessingham estate in the 1970s and for taking the trouble to look through boxes of old archives for photographs and paperwork relating to the sale. Since he kept a close eye on subsequent developments in the village, it is a shame that a fatal car accident in 2014 prevented him from seeing the publication of this book.

The practical advice and encouragement I have received from the authors of other books about the history of Norfolk – Margaret Bird and Elaine Murphy in particular, as well as the late Verily Anderson – has been tremendously helpful. The outstanding professionalism and dedication of the excellent team of archivists and volunteers at the Norfolk Record Office has made my research trips very enjoyable and I will miss spending long hours in the search room studying old maps and manuscripts. I would also like to thank the staff of the Norfolk Heritage Centre, the Norfolk Library Service, the Norfolk Historic Environment Service, the Round Tower Churches Society, the Ordnance Survey and the National Portrait Gallery for their assistance and for giving me permission to publish images from their collections. I am especially grateful to the late Dr. John Blatchly for allowing me to spend a couple of hours in the Ipswich School archives in search of information about Robert and Denham Spurrell and for his continued interest in my research afterwards. I am sorry he has not lived to see the completion of this book. I would also like to thank Ruth Bloom for finding and photographing documents for me at The National Archives in Kew.

Special thanks are due to Inge Spurrell and her late husband Richard for throwing open the doors of Thurgarton House and allowing me to look through old photograph albums and boxes of papers and letters, not to mention free roam of the house itself in search of clues to its architectural history. Their extraordinary hospitality during a number of extended visits and their detailed knowledge of the location of the graves, memorials and former homes of members of the Spurrell family will not be forgotten. I am also very grateful to my aunt and uncle, Caroline (née Spurrell) and Tony Dowson, for giving me my late grandfather's collection of photographs and family papers and for listening patiently ever since to enthusiastic reports of my latest genealogical findings.

This book would not have been possible were it not for the love, support and encouragement of my wife Abbey, and my deepest gratitude goes to her – particularly for visiting North Norfolk with me on several occasions, for proofreading my work and for taking care of the girls while I worked hard to finish the book.

I am also grateful to Hayley Meyer (née Finch) for offering to proofread the book and for her valuable assistance in the final stages of the project; and to my father-in-law Richard Pope for his helpful comments and support.

It only remains for me to thank Richard Pryor and Phillip Dickie of Barnwell Print for their help and advice in getting the book ready for printing. Any errors that remain in the text are entirely my own.

Jonathan Spurrell
August 2016

LIST OF ILLUSTRATIONS

Front cover: Field of barley in Bessingham – published by
    kind permission of Peter Wrighton
Back cover: 1988 aerial map of Norfolk - © Norfolk County
    Council
Map of Bessingham
North Norfolk coast photographed by F. C. J. Spurrell – ©
    Historic England
Postcard of Bessingham church
John Spurrell
Elizabeth Flaxman
Flaxman family memorial at Roughton church
Spurrell family memorial at Bessingham church
Roughton Mill – © Norfolk County Council
Charles Spurrell
Bessingham enclosure map – © Norfolk County Council
Drawing of Bessingham church by R. Ladbrooke – © Norfolk
    County Council
Daniel Spurrell
Flaxman Spurrell
Daniel and Sarah Frances Spurrell
Spurrell family at Faulkbourne Rectory
The Rev. Frederick Spurrell
The Rev. Charles Henry Spurrell
John Tuck outside the old Manor House – published by kind
    permission of Peter Wrighton
Plans of Bessingham church before and after its restoration –
    published by kind permission of the Norfolk Record Office
Bessingham Manor House – © Norfolk County Council
Drawing of Bessingham Manor House by the Rev. R. J.
    Simpson
Ordnance Survey map of Bessingham – © Ordnance Survey

The Mallett family – published by kind permission of Joyce
   Knowles
Agnes Finch – published by kind permission of George Finch
George Finch – published by kind permission of George Finch
Denham Spurrell, Mary Hitchcock and Mildred Spurrell
Ronald Hitchcock – published by kind permission of Sheridan
   Hughes
Claas combine harvester at Manor House Farm – published
   by kind permission of Peter Wrighton
Gordon Wrighton and Jack Wright – published by kind
   permission of Peter Wrighton
Myrtle Abigail – published by kind permission of Peter
   Wrighton

Colour plate
Bessingham church
The farmhouse at Manor House Farm – published by kind
   permission of Peter Wrighton
The former Horse Shoes Inn – published by kind permission
   of Peter Wrighton
Ruins of old farm buildings at Bessingham
Map showing the enclosure awards - published by kind
   permission of the Norfolk Record Office
Charles Spurrell by R. B. Joy
Catherine Case Copeman by Emily Scott
Stained glass window in Roughton church in memory of
   Sarah Joy – published by kind permission of the Round
   Tower Churches Society
Stained glass window in Bessingham church in memory of
   Daniel and Sarah Frances Spurrell – published by kind
   permission of the Round Tower Churches Society
Denham Spurrell with his dog Ruff by J. J. Shannon –
   published by kind permission of Sheridan Hughes
Narcissus 'Katherine Spurrell' – published by kind permission
   of the Royal Horticultural Society

Stained glass window in Bessingham church in memory of
Robert John Spurrell – published by kind permission of the
Round Tower Churches Society

Albert Finch by Mary l'Anson – published by kind permission
of George Finch

Yew Tree Cottage, Bessingham – published by kind
permission of Joyce Knowles

Fiddlers Haven, Bessingham – published by kind permission
of Peter Wrighton

1988 aerial map of Norfolk - © Norfolk County Council

Bessingham Manor House following years of neglect

Dining room of Bessingham Manor House

Tower at Bessingham Manor House – published by kind
permission of Peter Wrighton

Bessingham village sign – published by kind permission of
Peter Wrighton

Bessingham Manor House following its restoration –
published by kind permission of William and Dawn
Hickey

Bessingham church by Martin Sexton – published by kind
permission of Martin Sexton

MAP OF BESSINGHAM

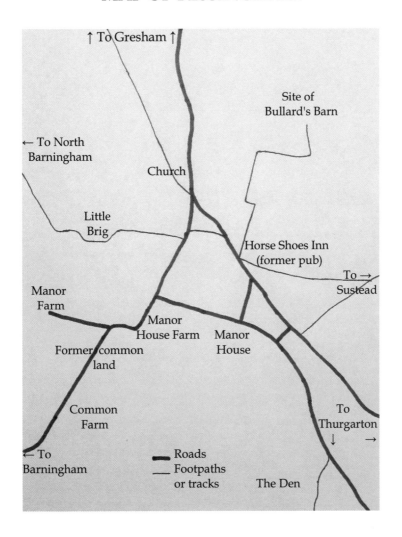

↑ To Gresham ↑

Site of
Bullard's Barn

← To North
Barningham

Church

Little
Brig

Horse Shoes Inn
(former pub)

To →
Sustead

Manor
Farm

Manor
House Farm

Manor
House

Former common
land

Common
Farm

To
Thurgarton
↓   →

← To
Barningham

▬▬ Roads
___ Footpaths
     or tracks

The Den

xvii

FAMILY TREES

1. Spurrell, Flaxman and Joy families (abridged)

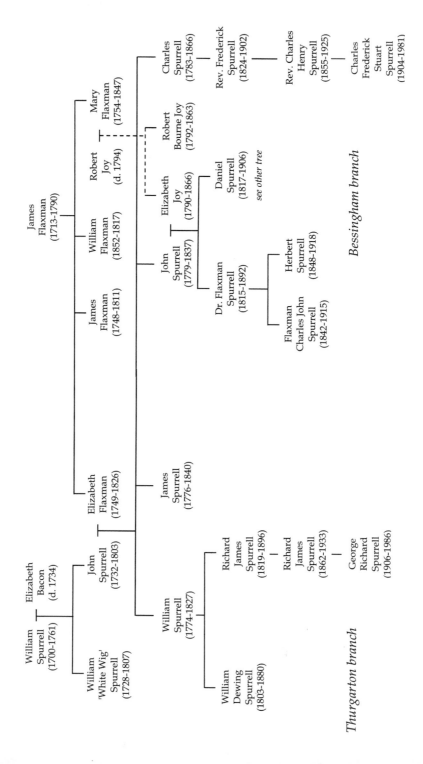

2. Daniel Spurrell's family (abridged)

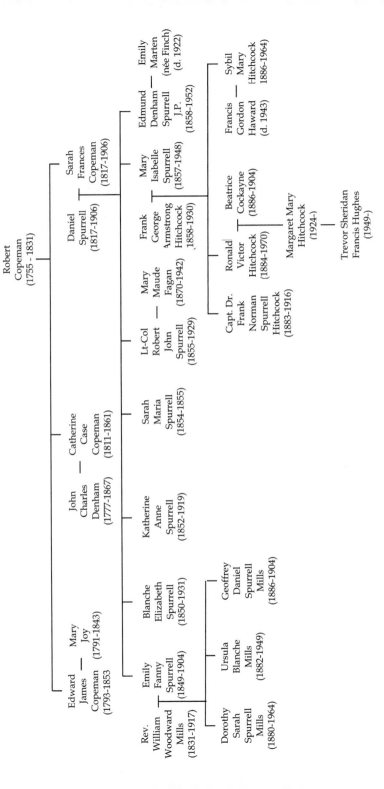

FOREWORD

By Shelagh Hutson
Chairman, Norfolk County Council (2011-2012)

I am delighted to have been asked to write this foreword, not least because of the extraordinary way in which Jonathan Spurrell traced me.

I was born in Cromer in early 1938, of parents who were at that time living with my widowed paternal grandmother, Catherine O'Connell, in a house in Bessingham then called The Den, but now renamed Elizabeth House.

My parents had met in India at an army garrison named Mhow, where my father was an officer and my mother a sister with Queen Alexandra's Royal Army Nursing Corps. Having resigned their commissions they had returned to England – actually 12 months apart – to marry early in 1936 and initially had no home of their own to go to. Their stay in Bessingham proved to be rather a longer-lasting temporary measure than originally intended, but following an interim short-term tenancy of the bungalow opposite the Links Hotel in West Runton, finally a permanent home was bought in the village of Hoe, in Mid Norfolk, just before the outbreak of the Second World War, when I was only about 18 months old.

I have always been interested in beautiful North Norfolk and regretted that my family moved away from that area. I took each of my parents on a tour round shortly before their deaths and had discussed my roots there with the late John Shrive, who had kindly offered to try to arrange a visit for me to Elizabeth House, before his untimely and tragic death in a road accident. I had also read with interest the coverage of the sale of Bessingham Manor House and its proposed restoration in the *Eastern Daily Press*.

It was a great surprise to me in 2012 when out of the blue I received an email from Jonathan Spurrell – that surname being one which I remembered being mentioned by my parents in the context of their time in North Norfolk. In his email Jonathan explained that he was carrying out research about the Bessingham estate for a book he was preparing to write and had found my name in the Bessingham baptism register. There would presumably also have been a mention of my slightly older brother Patrick who sadly died of leukaemia aged 32. Further research had revealed my married name and the fact that I was now Chairman of Norfolk County Council.

It was a further surprise to discover that Jonathan was living in America, near Washington, D. C., and was doing most of his research from there, but when he came to England a little while later I invited him to have lunch with me at County Hall. We have had occasional contact since.

Bessingham: The Story of a Norfolk Estate, 1766-1970 is of particular interest to me as I know little of my father's early life or his connection with North Norfolk. I do know he was born in Eastbourne, that his father had a Master's degree in languages from Pembroke College, Cambridge, and that apparently he ran a language school in Germany. I do not know why he was not in the army as generations of the family had been; my great-grandfather was a Major-General and I have his sword which is engraved with his name.

Tragically for my father, when he was six years old, his father died in his mid-forties from a duodenal ulcer. I do not know why they were then living in North Norfolk. Somewhere amongst my mother's effects I have seen a cutting about my grandfather's funeral which names the families represented and the wreaths received and stated that 'the widow was too distressed to attend'. I do know that my grandmother, for the rest of her life, always wore black and shut herself away from the world. I know little of what was obviously a difficult childhood for my father except that he talked of living at Sustead Old Hall, which I now know from Jonathan was owned by a member of the Spurrell family, as was The Den in Bessingham.

I have photographs taken on my christening day at The Den and I also remember paintings by my father's sister of the drive to the house.

This book, on which I must congratulate Jonathan for his detailed and meticulous research, is a fascinating read for me and I expect many others.

Shelagh Hutson
August 2016

INTRODUCTION

When my grandmother Mildred Spence left Norwich
High School in 1924 she asked some of her fellow pupils
to sign her autograph book. One of those pupils was
Constance Kingsmill, and although they did not stay in
touch to realise it, within ten years of leaving school they
had both married men from different branches of the
same Spurrell family. My grandfather, Charles Frederick
Stuart Spurrell, was the son of a clergyman and the
grandson of two clergymen. Their peripatetic careers
had taken them all over the country but they always
remained close to their relatives in Norfolk. Charles's
grandfather, the Rev. Frederick Spurrell, was asked by
his cousin Daniel Spurrell of Bessingham Manor House
to officiate at his wedding in 1848, and again at the
wedding of his eldest daughter in 1879. Frederick's
family were among the first visitors to the new Manor
House built in 1870, and during that visit his teenage son
became besotted with one of Daniel's daughters. Daniel's
family repaid the visit, and a photograph exists of his
children posing in front of Faulkbourne Rectory in Essex
in the 1880s after a game of tennis.

The visits continued into the twentieth century, by
which point Denham Spurrell had succeeded his father
Daniel at Bessingham Manor House. Charles and
Mildred stayed there in the mid-1930s, and my Aunt

Caroline remembers making the trip as a young girl in the 1940s.

A short distance from Bessingham Manor House is Thurgarton House, which in 1933 became the home of Constance Kingsmill's husband, George Spurrell. George and Charles were third cousins, but although Charles was in regular contact with relatives at Bessingham there is no evidence that he visited or even corresponded with the Thurgarton branch of the family. In fact, George had decided to leave the farm at Thurgarton in the hands of a caretaker while he and Constance lived in Africa, so when Charles and Mildred visited Bessingham in the 1930s my grandmother was unaware that her former classmate's home was so close*. It was only about five years ago that I found Mildred's autograph book and discovered this interesting connection.

After the Second World War the visits to Bessingham came to an end. Charles's career had taken him to London, where he worked in the Treasury Solicitor's Department from 1946 until his retirement in 1969. Charles and Mildred's holidays might include motoring around Norfolk and stopping to look at family graves and memorials at Bessingham church, as they did in 1967, but the condition of the village was very different from what they had seen before the war. In the intervening years Denham Spurrell had died and his heir, Ronald Hitchcock, decided not to live in Bessingham but to manage the estate from a distance. Bessingham had now become a 'ghost village' – its cottages mostly unoccupied

---

* Constance died in Africa in 1939, so there were no further opportunities for Mildred to meet her.

or derelict, its pub closed, and the Manor House silent and empty. Three years after Charles and Mildred's 1967 visit the estate was broken up and sold.

~

My grandfather died in January 1981, just a few months before I was born. It is a pity that I never knew him. I was interested in history at a very early age and he would have enjoyed sharing stories and anecdotes about the family, including his visits to Bessingham. But it was precisely because I did not know him (I knew my other three grandparents) that I was curious to discover more about his life and his ancestors. My father gave me Charles's copy of the family tree when I was a teenager and I enjoyed studying all the names and figuring out relationships. Later at university (studying languages, but always reading history books in my spare time) I began writing to distant family members and visiting libraries and record offices, building up a fuller picture of the lives of my forebears by uncovering their experiences, thoughts and interests.

I began wondering what I should do with all this information when in the summer of 2009 I heard that Bessingham Manor House was going to be put up for auction. By now, after decades of neglect, it had fallen into disrepair, and the prospect of its sale had created a great deal of local interest, including in the media. I realised that there might be other people who wanted to know more about the history of Bessingham Manor House and the people who lived and worked there.

I contacted the *North Norfolk News* to see if they would be willing to publish an article about my research, in which I might also appeal for information from anyone with stories about Bessingham's past. I was amazed at how large the response was. The article appeared in print on 11 March 2010 and within a week about a dozen people had sent me emails or letters. Others contacted me after the article was reprinted in the *Eastern Daily Press* on 20 March. I quickly realised that my research so far had only scratched the surface. It also became very clear that it was impossible to write an account of Bessingham Manor House and its inhabitants without exploring the wider context of the estate and the village.

Bessingham is a small village of 495 acres (about three-quarters of a square mile). For about 200 years before 1970 most of that land was owned and managed as a single estate, and most of the dwellings in the village were tied cottages belonging to the estate*. Therefore to talk of the estate or of the village is practically the same thing and the terms will be used interchangeably throughout this book.

~

The majority of people in England, especially in rural areas, were illiterate until the late nineteenth century. Primary education had become compulsory in the 1870s but was not properly enforced until the 1890s. Therefore almost all the records that exist before then were written by the gentry or the clergy, and the working class perspective is often unavailable to historians. From the 1890s onwards new opportunities emerged for working men and women to have a say in local affairs through the

---

* Historians call this type of village a 'closed village'.

medium of the newly established parish and district councils. The landlords' hegemony was gradually being eroded.

Nevertheless, landlords remained influential in village affairs well into the twentieth century. Their attitudes and behaviour could greatly affect the mood in the village, and if they were unkind or illiberal it could lead to strikes or violent action. The picture that emerges in Bessingham, though, is one in which the relationship between landlord and tenant was for the most part cordial and born of mutual trust and respect. Instances of kindness by both Daniel and Denham Spurrell are not difficult to find, and although reports of their deeds in parish magazines and local newspapers often contained more than a trace of deference or sycophancy, there are enough examples of the family's generosity for us to conclude that Bessingham's landlords were generally held in high regard by their tenants. They forgave loans, allowed rent to be paid late, and prevented orphans in the village from being sent to the workhouse by giving them a home at the Manor House. Unlike employers in the burgeoning towns and cities of Victorian England, rural employers saw their workers and tenants on a more regular basis and could see if they were struggling. This is particularly true of a small village such as Bessingham, where most people had some connection with the estate.

It is with affection that many people today who are in their 70s and 80s remember Denham Spurrell. The inherent unfairness of the old landlord system is apparent to modern observers, with its lack of social mobility and the enormous disparity between the amount of work done by the landlord and the benefits he received, but many at the time found that it was a system that worked, especially when the landlord showed genuine concern for the welfare of his tenants. Everyone in the village was wedded to the system: their livelihoods depended on the prosperity and sustainability of the estate. The labourers worked long hours in the fields to provide for their families, and the landlord relied on cheap and plentiful labour and good grain prices to support his lifestyle and leisure pursuits. On a small estate such as Bessingham, where the labourer's and landlord's families had lived and worked alongside each other for generations, the landlord was also directly involved in the day-to-day running of the farm. Daniel was out in the fields during the harvest and at other times. He kept records of the crops being grown in each field and lists of the animals on the farm, as well as account books showing the work done by the labourers day after day, year after year. This repeating cycle of agricultural activity, interspersed with celebrations and tragedies, was the basis for everyone's life in the village.

~

These labour account books, which give a fascinating and detailed description of the work done on the estate between the 1840s and the 1920s, are kept at the Norfolk Record Office (N.R.O.). This book would not have been possible without the vast collection of family, legal, agricultural, manorial and other records held at the N.R.O. I have also studied maps, drawings, photographs and printed works in libraries and museums in Norfolk and elsewhere, as well as a number of private collections that I am grateful to have been given permission to consult. The most enjoyable and rewarding part of my research has been the interviews and correspondence with people who either grew up in Bessingham or are connected with the village in other ways. Their anecdotes and recollections have helped to bring certain characters to life and I am very much aware that this book is a collaborative effort in which I am just one of the suppliers of information.

The long process of absorbing all this information about a miniscule area of the world – less than one square mile – has given me a better appreciation of the richness and complexity of the British countryside: layer upon layer of history that has left its mark on our environment and created the landscape we see around us today. In the modern age, when great distances can be covered quickly by car, it is easy to overlook the little details in the landscape, but every field, every lane, every hedgerow, every cottage and every church tower has a story to tell. Looking at old manuscripts has been an essential part of my research, but it has been equally important to walk along Bessingham's lanes and footpaths, stopping to notice the location of a hedgerow or a line of trees, in order to become more aware of and connected with the place I have been researching. And for me that connection is especially important because of my family's long association with this small patch of earth.

Britain is still fascinated by the countryside even though most of us now live in towns and cities. Or perhaps it is precisely because most of us now live in towns and cities that we have this strong fascination. The writer William Cobbett remarked as far back as 1833 that we are all 'deserters from the plough'[1] and ever since there has been a yearning to reconnect with the earth. Television and radio programmes about rural life –

whether contemporary or historical – are hugely popular, and for many people they offer an opportunity to connect vicariously with the countryside, even if it is sometimes portrayed as being more idyllic than it really is or was.

In a book such as this it is important to separate historical fact from rosy retrospection, and I hope to have achieved this, remaining unbiased when discussing my own ancestors. While the book will appeal mainly to those whose families live or lived in Bessingham, I hope that other people with an interest in the social history and landscape of Norfolk will also be tempted to pick up a copy.

Jonathan Spurrell
August 2016

The whole place is so heavy with history that in certain moods it gives you the feeling that you have but to put out your finger to touch the past[2].

~

Lilias Rider Haggard, *A Norfolk Notebook*

PART ONE

BEFORE 1766

Chapter 1

BASA'S PEOPLE

The fate of any farming community depends on the condition of the soil as well as on social, political and economic factors. For centuries Norfolk was one of the wealthiest counties in England and one of the most prolific in terms of agricultural production. The north of the county was long ago found to be ideal for arable farming, and the rich, loamy soil around Bessingham is no exception.

The village sits on the south-facing slopes of Cromer Ridge, an 'attractive, low, hilly landscape'[3] in what is otherwise a famously flat county. The ridge was formed after several waves of glaciers petered out near what is now the North Norfolk coast, leaving behind a huge pile of sand and gravel. The ridge stretches almost ten miles from Sidestrand to Holt and contains the county's highest point at Beacon Hill (102 metres above sea level) in West Runton.

Shortly before the end of the last Ice Age, meltwater flowed over the Cromer Ridge, allowing sand and flint gravel to trickle down into the small valleys to the south, creating the landscape in which places like Bessingham, Gresham, Thurgarton and Sustead now sit.

1

The earliest inhabitants of the region around Bessingham could have walked to the top of Cromer Ridge and seen Doggerland stretching out far beyond the northern horizon. The present coastline was established about 6,000 years ago after a rise in sea levels, but coastal erosion continues to have an impact on the landscape, with prehistoric sites such as Seahenge and more recently mediaeval towns such as Shipden being lost to the waves.

A photograph of the North Norfolk coast taken from Cromer Ridge in the late nineteenth century by Flaxman C. J. Spurrell.

These early settlers followed wild cattle and other animals, gradually clearing the forests and creating small farming communities. As they ploughed the fields they removed small stones and flints from the earth and later used them for building. Occasionally larger stones that had been transported by the glaciers were found. The Victorian geologist Clement Reid described a 'granitic rock'[4] about 2 ½ feet in width that had ended its Ice Age journey near Bessingham church. We know little about the lives of these early settlers but they have left some clues behind. Axeheads, daggers, coins and beads have all been unearthed in the area, including a prehistoric pebble mace head found in Bessingham.

Despite being so close to the coast, the land around Bessingham drains in the opposite direction. Small streams, or becks, combine to form Scarrow Beck, which joins the Bure near Aylsham and flows through the Broads before reaching the sea at Gorleston near Great Yarmouth. The source of the beck that passes through Bessingham is to the north-west of the village and marks the boundary between Gresham and North Barningham. It crosses Little Brig Lane and The Street, flows across what was once the parkland around the Manor House, and eventually becomes the boundary between Bessingham and Aldborough. It then leaves the village, tracing the boundary between Aldborough and Thurgarton. On most of its journey through Bessingham the beck flows in straight lines. This is evidence of earlier generations adapting the landscape to suit their agricultural needs since it was much easier to manoeuvre heavy ploughs and teams of oxen along straight field boundaries. The fact that the Aldborough-Thurgarton boundary zigzags very close to the straight beck suggests that the stream was straightened after the creation of parish boundaries in the Saxon period.

On the eve of the Roman invasion of Britain the Iceni inhabited the area now covered by Norfolk. They farmed the land and apart from Boudicca's revolt in A.D. 60-61 the transition to Roman rule was largely peaceful. Most of the Roman armies were concentrated along the Empire's borders such as Hadrian's Wall, so the military presence in Norfolk would have been minimal. The land was divided into estates, or villas, which grew crops for the local population as well as supplying the campaigning armies.

We know that the Romans were in Bessingham. In 1870 the Rev. H. T. Griffith wrote to the Society of Antiquaries announcing the discovery of Roman pottery in the north-west of the parish:

> I write to apprise you of a slight discovery of Roman remains in the parish of Bessingham, about 6 miles to the S.W. from Cromer. Some workmen in the employ of Daniel Spurrell, Esq. (the principal landed proprietor in the parish), were engaged in sinking a sand-pit on that gentleman's estate, when they came upon various fragments of Roman pottery, about 4 feet below the surface of the ground.
>
> These fragments are principally of the common blue clay, and perfectly plain; one or two of them however are of a finer clay, of a brown colour, and having the sides ribbed or fluted spirally. There is no whole vessel remaining, and the various portions appear to be those of cups or other small vessels.
>
> This discovery, trivial as it may appear, is so far interesting, as confirmatory evidence that Bessingham was once in Roman occupation, a fact which has been shown by remains of somewhat similar description having been not unfrequently turned up

during the last twenty years; and amongst others the almost perfect half of a Roman hand-mill[5].

The preservation of ancient remains was somewhat haphazard in the mid-nineteenth century when serious archaeology was still very much in its infancy, and it is not known what happened to these artefacts. But they were not the only Roman discoveries in Bessingham. Bricks and other objects were occasionally ploughed up and reused in new buildings. If you look closely at the walls of the church you can see a few Roman bricks that were inserted either at the time of construction or during later repairs. Recent discoveries of a Roman figurine, a pot and several coins have also been recorded by Norfolk County Council's Historic Environment Service, and there are almost certainly more artefacts waiting to be unearthed.

A few years after the 1870 discovery in Bessingham the archaeologist Flaxman C. J. Spurrell[*] was involved in recording the discovery of several thousand Roman coins in Baconsthorpe. The hoard had been found in a pot just below the surface, which a labourer had broken open when ploughing. He took some of the 'green buttons'[6] home to show his wife, who told him what they really were. Flaxman dated most of them to the third century A.D., and the 563 coins he kept for himself were donated to the Norwich Castle Museum after his death.

By the time the last Roman soldiers left Britain in the early fifth century, a flourishing Romano-British culture had developed and their departure would only have

---

[*] Daniel Spurrell's nephew.

been noticed on an administrative level. Angles and Saxons soon arrived from the continent to fill the void, trading and eventually intermarrying with the existing populations. Farming became more locally focused since it was no longer necessary to feed large imperial armies. The Roman villa system gradually broke down and new administrative structures emerged.

We do not know what name the Romans or Iceni used for the place we now call Bessingham (or Bassingham, as it was usually spelled until the mid-nineteenth century). It is generally agreed that the modern name refers to Basa, the Anglo-Saxon chieftain who decided to settle here after the Romans left. It has therefore been known for roughly fifteen hundred years as the 'home of Basa's people', from the Old English *Basa* + *ingas* (the people of) + *ham* (settlement)*. The neighbouring village of Thurgarton, whose history is closely connected with that of Bessingham, points to the influence of later Viking settlers. It is a combination of the Old Norse name *Thorgeirr* and the Old English word *tun*, meaning settlement or enclosure.

A Saxon brooch, bridle bit and strap ends have all been found in Bessingham, but the most important legacy from this period is the round bell tower at the west end of the church. England is home to almost two hundred round tower churches, about two-thirds of which are in Norfolk. It used to be thought that they had a defensive

---

* Francis Blomefield's theory, mentioned in *An Essay Towards A Topographical History of the County of Norfolk* (1808, vol. 8), namely that the word Bassingham describes a low lying *(base)* meadow *(ing)*, does not seem to be shared by other place name historians.

role, but the consensus now is that they were originally built to house the bells and have never had any other purpose. The reason they are round is that there is not much stone in East Anglia and it is easier to build round towers than square ones when large stones are not available. Round towers are also found in Scandinavia and northern Germany, so it is possible that the Saxons were influenced by contemporary church-builders on the continent.

An early twentieth-century postcard of Bessingham church, showing its Saxon round tower.

The material we see in Bessingham's church tower is ferricrete – also called puddingstone, ironstone or iron-bound conglomerate. There are four distinct layers of ferricrete, probably corresponding to four separate periods of construction. It is a fairly young stone, a combination of sand and gravel cemented by iron minerals to form a hard rock. Modern geologists cannot find it in the ground in Norfolk, and its widespread use in church towers suggests it was a popular building material that has been depleted.

Bessingham's church tower dates from the eleventh century and is therefore one of the oldest belfries in the county. It stands at the highest point in the village, commanding views over the surrounding countryside, and was probably built on the site of an earlier wooden church. Perhaps, even before that, the prominent hilltop location served as a prehistoric sacred site.

'Norfolk would not be Norfolk without a church tower on the horizon or round a corner up a lane'[7], wrote John Betjeman – and Bessingham is no exception. Within about a one-mile radius of Bessingham church are four more: North Barningham, Thurgarton with its thatched roof, and Gresham and Sustead with their round towers. This part of Norfolk contains a cluster of round tower churches at Bessingham, Gresham, Sustead, Aylmerton, Roughton, Matlaske, Thwaite and Wickmere. Situated along quiet country lanes, they are very much part of the distinctive North Norfolk landscape, especially as they were built by local hands using local materials. The pleasant, undulating countryside, with its patchwork of fields and woods, quiet villages and old farmhouses, makes this an extremely attractive part of the county, with a tremendously rich cultural heritage, and its identity becomes clearer as we move into the Norman age.

Chapter 2

LORDS OF THE MANOR

Twenty years after the Norman Conquest of 1066, William I commissioned a survey of his new kingdom to determine the amount of taxes owed to the crown. For historians the resulting publication, known as Domesday Book, provides vital information about land ownership in the early days of Norman rule. Under the newly imposed feudal system, all land in England belonged to the king, who granted manors to individual tenants-in-chief – an act known as enfeoffment.

William gave the manor of Bessingham to Drogo de la Beuvrière, a Flemish soldier who had fought alongside him at the Battle of Hastings. Drogo was rewarded with large tracts of land in Lincolnshire and Yorkshire, as well as a handful of manors in Norfolk, including Bessingham, North Barningham and Erpingham. Bessingham had been forfeited by Edric of Laxfield, one of the largest Saxon overlords in East Anglia before 1066.

According to Domesday Book, Bessingham was small in comparison with many of the surrounding villages. It contained sixteen households and had a taxation value of 1 geld unit. In 1086 the lord of the manor received a total of £3 in rent from his tenants, compared with £1 twenty years earlier. There were three plough teams (each of eight oxen), one of which belonged to the lord of the manor and two to the rest of the village[8].

The history of Bessingham over the next few centuries is essentially a list of the lords of the manor since very little else exists in the way of records. The de Basingham family were enfeoffed with the manor and held it until the thirteenth century when Sir Walter de Mautby inherited the land from his father-in-law, Sir Piers de Basingham. In 1440 Sir John Mautby's daughter and heiress, Margaret, married John Paston and Bessingham became one of the many possessions of that well-known family. The Pastons already owned several manors in North Norfolk, as well as Gresham Castle to the north of Bessingham. They are remembered today for the letters they wrote in the fifteenth century, which offer a unique view of the experiences of a leading Norfolk family at the time. John Paston was a lawyer who spent considerable amounts of time in London, leaving Margaret to run his Norfolk estates. One of the most notable events in her life was the attack on Gresham Castle by Lord Moleyns in 1450. Moleyns disputed the Pastons' ownership of the manor of Gresham and attacked the castle with a thousand men[*]. John was away and Margaret and her soldiers barricaded themselves inside, successfully fighting off the attackers. Many years later, when Margaret died in 1484, she left 8d to every household in Bessingham[9].

~

---

[*] Thomas Chaucer, Speaker of the House of Commons and son of the famous poet, had acquired the manor of Gresham from Lord Moleyns and sold it to the Pastons.

The village grew throughout the Middle Ages and the patchwork of fields and lanes that we know today was established. The earliest Ordnance Survey maps show oaks and oak stumps along the parish boundaries. These were important landmarks in the village and parishioners would 'beat the bounds' every year, keeping an eye out for evidence that neighbouring parishes were encroaching on their land. The fact that the Ordnance Survey included these ancient oaks on maps in the early 1900s implies that they still had some significance for the rural population. Encroachments took place in the village too and both Edward Crogate and Robert Mary were brought before the manorial court in the early 1600s for allegedly allowing their animals to trespass on other people's land.

There is a reference to a fair being held at a place called Bassingham Wongs during the reign of Elizabeth I. Fairs were often used by the lord of the manor to raise money and for this fair he levied a fee of 9s 8d[10].

As the village grew, so did the church. In the thirteenth century the chancel was added and in the next century the porch was built. Above the entrance to the porch is a niche, surrounded by Roman tiles, which originally contained the statue of a saint. This may well be the fifteenth-century oak figure that the Rev. Frederick Spurrell exhibited in Chelmsford in 1875, although its subsequent whereabouts are unknown.

The church, which is dedicated to St. Mary the Virgin, has a silver communion cup, dated 1657, that is inscribed 'Basyingham Seynct Andrew'. This suggests that after the Reformation the dedication was changed by a Puritan clergyman or a puritanical congregation who were uncomfortable with the reference to the Virgin Mary. Their iconoclasm also involved removing images of the seven sacraments from the font. Whereas the dedication was later reverted to St. Mary, the damage to the font was irreparable and to this day its sides remain plain. The church's treble bell dates from around this time and is inscribed 'Charles Newman made mee – 1699,' while the tenor bell is probably about 250 years older.

~

The Pastons continued to hold the manor of Bessingham in the seventeenth century and in 1679 Sir Robert Paston was elevated to the peerage as Earl of Yarmouth. On the second Earl's death in 1732 his Norfolk estates were purchased by Admiral George Anson, and within a few decades the Ansons, whose family seat was at Shugborough Hall in Staffordshire, began selling off some of their Norfolk possessions.

By the late seventeenth century names such as Bacon, Bond, England, Spurrell and Thaxter begin to appear in the lists of tenants – names that crop up frequently as the number of surviving historical records increases. In 1751 Thomas Frankland first appears in the manorial documents when he was admitted to a piece of copyhold land. The Franklands lived at what is now Manor House Farm and erected at least two barns. On one Thomas placed his initials on the exterior wall and carved 'TF 1757' on a beam inside. The other barn was demolished but a wooden beam bearing the date 1747 was moved to a new barn, erected in 1874.

Other records from this period include the churchwardens' and overseers' accounts. The churchwardens' expenses included everyday items such as a new broom (costing 2d in 1709) and maintenance of the church and churchyard. A 'lock and kee'[11] were repaired for one shilling in 1764. There were costs relating to church services too. Sixpence was paid for a new prayer book in 1709 and again in 1756. Bread and wine were usually distributed only twice a year, at Christmas and Easter, costing two shillings each time. In 1729 the churchwarden Charles England paid a boy two shillings for catching 24 caddows*, and four years later he paid someone five shillings for catching a fox.

The overseers collected rates from the farmers and landowners and distributed them among the poor of the village. In 1757 their expenses included six shillings of firewood for the widow Shepherd; later in the year they paid for the cost of her burial. Ann Youngman received two bushels of coal and various items of clothing, including an apron, 'anchorchief'[12], gown, petticoat and stockings.

In 1765 John Spurrell was chosen as churchwarden of Bessingham. His expenses for that year included bread and wine, not only at Christmas and Easter but also at Whitsuntide, as well as 1s 6d for cleaning the church and 3s 6d for washing the surplice. Over the previous few years John, a bachelor in his thirties, had acquired various parcels of copyhold land in Bessingham, but the following year he purchased a freehold estate called The Wood and laid the foundations of his family's prosperity.

---

* Jackdaws.

13

PART TWO

1766 ~ 1840

Chapter 3

UNCOMFORTABLE RELATIONS

The Spurrells were by no means newcomers to the Bessingham scene. The branch that established itself at Bessingham was an offshoot of a family that had lived in neighbouring Thurgarton since Tudor times. William, Joan, Nicholas, John and Robert Sporrell all appear on the opening pages of the Thurgarton baptism registers in the 1530s*. Their parents, William and Agnes, died in 1558 and 1559 respectively and may have been kin to another William Sporrell whose will was proved in 1506.

It has been suggested that the Sporrells moved to Thurgarton from Norwich and may have been related to William de Sporle, a leading figure in Norwich in the second half of the fourteenth century[13]. He became a freeman of the city in 1349 and in the 1370s had the important job of overseeing all the food for sale at Norwich market. He was treasurer of Norwich in 1390-1391 and later sat on a committee that considered the creation of the office of mayor. He was buried at St. John Timberhill in the city[14]. His name suggests that his ancestors may have come from Sporle, a village near Swaffham that was home to a Benedictine priory from

---

* The spelling changed from Sporrel(l) to Spurrell in the seventeenth century.

1123 to 1414. Other de Sporles and Sporrells can be found in Norwich in the fifteenth century, although no connection has ever been confirmed between them and the Thurgarton family.

The Spurrells lived in the northernmost part of Thurgarton, where it juts out towards Gresham. Their farm extended into Bessingham, Sustead and Gresham, and by the seventeenth century they had also acquired land in Erpingham. Family wills refer to various parcels of land in Bessingham. The will of one William Spurrell, who died in 1663, mentions a meadow adjoining 'Smiths Hirne Lane'[15], the track leading from Bessingham to Aldborough Hall which later became the driveway to The Den (now Elizabeth House).

By the late seventeenth century the family were wealthy enough to commission family portraits by London artists. One painting by Theodore Russel, showing 'Miss Spurrell' – almost certainly Hannah Spurrell – in a blue and orange dress with pearls in her hair, was painted in the 1680s and remained with the Bessingham Spurrells until it was sold at Sotheby's in 1930.

Hannah's father, who died in 1707, left his property in Thurgarton and the surrounding area to his son Joseph, who served as churchwarden of Bessingham for several years. Joseph died shortly afterwards and bequeathed the estate to his young son William. Since William was still a minor, his mother Rachel was directed to manage the property until he reached the age of twenty-one. Joseph also left land to his daughters, including two enclosures of about four acres in Bessingham that he had purchased from Thomas Newman for £50 in 1693, which he gave to his daughter Elizabeth.

William did not want to wait until his twenty-first birthday to take over his father's property. He was an ambitious young man and at the age of 18 he signed an agreement with his mother allowing him to occupy and manage the Thurgarton estate in exchange for an annual payment to his mother of £14. This annuity was to be handed over in two instalments – on Lady Day and Michaelmas – at the south porch of Thurgarton church.

William soon began improving and expanding the estate and establishing himself as one of the leading yeoman farmers in the area. In 1722 he is recorded as leasing a house, outbuildings and seventeen acres in Thurgarton from William Daniel of Mannington for a period of twenty years at £16 4s per year. He was also the first of several generations of Spurrells to serve as Chief Constable of North Erpingham hundred, a position that involved being responsible for keeping the peace and collecting rates*.

William married Elizabeth Bacon, the daughter of another family of prosperous Thurgarton farmers. The Bacons lived next to Thurgarton church, on the site of what is now Thurgarton Hall. The Bacon and Spurrell families had already intermarried in 1618 and William re-established the link by marrying Elizabeth just over a century later. She gave birth to five sons, but three of them died before reaching their first birthdays. The two surviving sons, William and John, would one day own

---

*Hundreds were administrative areas that existed from the late Saxon period until the nineteenth century, when they were succeeded by poor law unions, sanitary unions and, most importantly, rural district councils. North Erpingham hundred contained 32 parishes.

several hundred acres between them in Thurgarton and Bessingham.

In 1733, the year after John was born, his father rebuilt the family home, Thurgarton House*. This was a time when yeomen farmers were replacing or extending their houses as the rural economy entered a new phase of prosperity. William's new house was built of red brick and flint with six windows on the south-facing façade, three on each side of the front door. When the house was extended in the mid-nineteenth century, the original façade on the front of the house was hidden behind a new layer of yellow bricks that were more popular with the Victorians. To save money, however, the red bricks and flint on the side and rear of the house were not covered up since they were not visible from the lane. The new house was a sign of William's aspirations for his family, a bold mark on the landscape that reflected his confidence and his position in local society.

William wrote his will in August 1760, 'being sick and weak in body but of sound mind, memory and understanding (blessed be God therefore)'[16], dividing his property between his two surviving sons. To the eldest, William (whom we shall refer to by his nickname 'White Wig' from now on to avoid confusion with the many other Williams in the family), he bequeathed 'all and singular my messuages, lands, tenements and hereditaments situate, lying and being in Thurgarton,

---

* For much of the twentieth century it was called Thurgarton Old Hall and before that a number of historical documents refer to it as Thurgarton Hall, although it should not be confused with the former Bacon residence of the same name located next to Thurgarton church.

Bassingham, Gresham and Sustead,' which is legal jargon for the Thurgarton estate. John meanwhile received 'all and singular my messuages, lands, tenements and hereditaments situate, lying and being in Erpingham and Thwaite'[17]. Within a few months of writing his will, William died and his sons penned an affectionate tribute to him and their mother, who had died when they were still boys. Anyone who has walked up the aisle of Thurgarton church will have stepped over these words:

He was a Father to the Fatherless,
He helped the Widdows in their Distress,
He never was given to Worldly Pride,
He Liv'd an honest man and so he dy'd.
They was tender parents, our Loss was great,
We hope they both eternal Joy will meet.

~

As well as inheriting land in Erpingham and Thwaite, John also acquired his father's ambitious nature and it was not long before he began buying up parcels of land in the area. Fortunately for him, families such as the Ansons were selling off property at this time and yeoman farmers like John were snapping it up, often helped by other landowners who provided mortgages. John was aided in his acquisition of the Bessingham estate by James Flaxman, who lived in Roughton at what is now called Flaxman's Farm. James had already given loans to several people in Bessingham and in 1766 John took out a £1,800 mortgage with him and moved to his new estate called The Wood*.

John immediately got involved in village affairs. In 1765 he had been elected churchwarden and held this position until his death almost 40 years later. In 1766 he paid for carpenters, bricklayers, painters and glaziers to work on the church, as well as 2s 3d for a new bell rope in 1767 and £1 11s for cloth to make a surplice, communion cloth and napkin in 1794.

He also served as an overseer of the poor and as the largest ratepayer in the village he no doubt wanted to make sure he had a say in how the money was being spent. Before the workhouse system was established in the nineteenth century, each village was responsible for its own paupers and provided them with clothing, fuel or money for rent. In 1777, for example, the overseers spent several pounds on items for Robert Thaxter, including shoes for his family; and in 1803 they paid Sarah Frankland 17s 4d for John Harper's half-year rent.

On 9 May 1771 John Spurrell married James Flaxman's eldest daughter, Elizabeth, who was seventeen years his junior. As we shall see later on, the advantages of this marriage continued to be felt by the Spurrells for decades

---

* As we have already seen with Thurgarton House, property names are not permanent and sometimes several names were in use at the same time. The Bessingham estate was usually called The Wood in the late eighteenth and early nineteenth centuries. The name was still in use in the 1870s, even after the new Manor House was built. The Manor House itself is also called Bessingham Hall in some historical records, but unless quoting directly from those documents it will be referred to as Bessingham Manor House throughout this book.

to come. This is because most of the Flaxman wealth and property was eventually left to the Spurrells. As with the Bacon family, the Flaxmans and Spurrells had been united in marriage once before, when James's great-great-uncle Robert Flaxman married Margaret Spurrell at Thurgarton in 1583. James was born at Hempstead but spent most of his life in Roughton. He also owned land in Felbrigg, Northrepps and Southrepps, and through his wife Mary Ellis the family acquired additional land in Sidestrand. James had done well for himself. On his death he left the large sum of £1,400 to his daughter Elizabeth Spurrell and divided his property between his sons James and William.

John Spurrell and Elizabeth Flaxman.

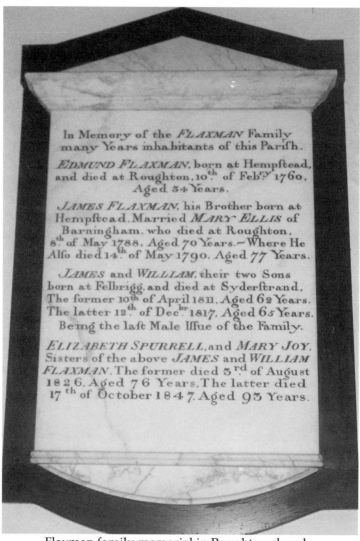

In Memory of the *FLAXMAN* Family
many Years inhabitants of this Parifh.

EDMUND FLAXMAN, born at Hempftead,
and died at Roughton, 10th of Febry 1760,
Aged 54 Years.

JAMES FLAXMAN, his Brother born at
Hempftead. Married *MARY ELLIS* of
Barningham. who died at Roughton,
8th of May 1788. Aged 70 Years.—Where He
Alfo died 14th of May 1790. Aged 77 Years.

JAMES and *WILLIAM*, their two Sons
born at Felbrigg, and died at Syderftrand,
The former 10th of April 1811. Aged 62 Years.
The latter 12th of Decbr 1817. Aged 65 Years.
Being the laft Male Iffue of the Family.

ELIZABETH SPURRELL, and *MARY JOY*,
Sisters of the above *JAMES* and *WILLIAM*
FLAXMAN. The former died 3rd of August
1826. Aged 76 Years. The latter died
17 th of October 1847. Aged 93 Years.

Flaxman family memorial in Roughton church.

James Flaxman's eldest son, also called James, lived in Sidestrand and in 1806 a local writer noted that, 'Upon

24

this delightful spot a very good house has lately been erected by Mr. James Flaxman'[18]. The house was called Sidestrand Lodge (now Hall) and when James died he directed that the Lodge and the surrounding 140 acre estate be sold, but that if one of his nephews wanted it they could purchase it for £5,000. It was his sister's son John Spurrell, who three years earlier had inherited the Bessingham estate, who decided to buy it. James's younger brother William died in 1817, leaving his land in Roughton and Felbrigg to the Joy family (see end of chapter). He also owned a farm in Pennsylvania, which he gave to his nephew Charles Spurrell*.

John and Elizabeth had four boys and four girls: Elizabeth (1772), William (1774), James (1776), John (1779), Mary (1781), Charles (1783), Sarah (1786) and Frances (1788). William, their first-born son, was educated at Cromer, and his school book from 1792 includes notes on a variety of topics such as 'On the Necessity of Youth in Generally Acquiring Knowledge' (1 June 1792) and 'On the Gratitude of Scholars Towards their Teachers' (4 June 1792). William kept the books and used the empty pages after leaving school, since paper was not cheap. In the summer of 1796 he copied out a 'Hymn to the Creator for the Present Seasonable Weather'. He also jotted down a recommendation for a servant, warning that although he was not a drinker he did encourage others to drink – but on balance William found him to be a good servant. Other pages show William's accounts with stationers and merchants in Norfolk and London and drafts of letters he sent.

---

* My great-great-great-grandfather. Charles sold the 169 acre farm a few years later.

In 1802 William moved into Thurgarton House. His uncle, White Wig, intended to leave the estate to him and William learned how to run it under his uncle's guidance. White Wig was a difficult man, though, and lived in a separate part of the house from William. William recorded that his uncle was 'continuing in the same manner'[19] as before, which was probably not intended as a compliment. Shortly before this, William's sister Mary had become pregnant as the result of a relationship with the stable boy, John Stokes. The family sought to protect Mary and her reputation, and in a copy of a letter that William jotted down in his old school book he offered his own thoughts on Mary's condition with brotherly compassion:

> I must beg to say a word in her favour, poor thing. Young as she is and shut up from the world, she certainly was an easier prey to the evil she must endure, encouraged by the villain's treachery and evil dictates, by dread of the awful hour of discovery. She then kept her secret, now openly exposed to shame and disgrace, [and] is left with the melancholy reflection of being deceived – and deceiving all who were most dear to her[20].

William noted that Mary's condition was 'generally suspected and believed in the neighbourhood but [her] residence is known by none but the family'. It was to her Aunt Mary at Roughton Mill that she had been sent before being moved on. William heard that Stokes was working in Aylmerton but he had not seen him since

Mary went away. Such situations were by no means uncommon. Aunt Mary told William about 'one in the neighbourhood near here of rather high degree who at this time is under the unfortunate disaster of the same nature ... by her father's coachman'. Mary gave birth to a daughter, Emily Rose, and later married Robert Bond, a farmer from Erpingham. William commented that 'this last plan of marriage was certainly a better one than the first proceedings by living with him as housekeeper unmarried'. Robert and Mary went on to have nine children of their own and both lived into their 80s*.

In an undated letter to his brother James, William described their father's declining health:

> I fear his ill health is rather of serious consequence and has given us much concern from being poorly near three months. The disorder first began with a swelling in the neck though without being tender or giving much pain, rather an obstruction in eating and speaking, and so continued unaccounted for, tho' have had the best advise, from so long being poorly and loss of appetite has render'd our Father

---

* I do not know if Robert and Mary brought up Emily, but she was not forgotten by the family (Mary's parents both left her money in their wills). Later Emily married Richard Smith, a veterinary surgeon in Aylsham. Twenty years later Mary's sister Sarah also had an illegitimate child, fathered by George Pank, a surveyor from Cromer, but her fate was more tragic: she spent the remaining thirty years of her life in a private lunatic asylum in Heigham, near Norwich.

very feble that we now earnestly hope and pray for a spedy recovery – the doctors say but little on the matter[21].

On 24 January 1803 William wrote again to James as their father's condition deteriorated:

Knowing your anxiety to hear the state of our dear Fathers disorder, I think it a duty incumbent on me to communicate what so dearly concerns us, the welfare of so kind a parent as dear Father who I am sorry yet in despair in spite of all the efforts that have been us'd to recover him the doctors seem baffled with the disorder and are at a loss to know how to remove the complaint which lies apparently wholy in the neck which now causes a cough and raising with much difficulty. I hope nothing will be spar'd that can be thought to do any service and I don't think it is so. Dr. Lubbock and other Norwich [doctors] have been consulted but none speak encourageably on the case[22].

One month later their father passed away. He was buried at Bessingham in a brick vault near the church door. He had written his will in 1802. With his eldest son William in line to inherit the Thurgarton estate from White Wig, and two of his sons having embarked on other careers, John left the Bessingham estate to his third son, John. He also made bequests to various family members, not forgetting his illegitimate granddaughter, Emily Rose Spurrell, who received £100. He added that he had already spent £50 towards the 'advancement in life'[23] of his son James and £250 for Charles, and had taken this into account when writing his will. James was working for the London brewers Barclay Perkins & Co. (see Chapter 4) and in 1802 Charles became sixth mate aboard the Henry Addington, marking the beginning of a decade-long career in the merchant navy that took him to both the East and West Indies before he returned to terra firma and joined his brother James at the brewery.

~

White Wig died in 1807. He had held respectable positions in the neighbourhood as Chief Constable of North Erpingham hundred and churchwarden of Thurgarton, but his family sometimes found his behaviour infuriating. His nephew James, referring to one example of obstinacy in 1805, described him as an:

> unaffectionate, hard hearted Uncle, who as well from his past, as his present conduct, seems destitute of all moral probity, and whose thoughts appear employed only to make all his relations he has to do with uncomfortable, this is known, for he has shewn it in too many instances and now again to William, who I am glad has consulted his Uncle Flaxmans and I shall be extremely glad to hear that my Uncle Spurrell's conduct bears a different aspect, though I think myself he never will reform unless dreams of his black deeds affright him[24].

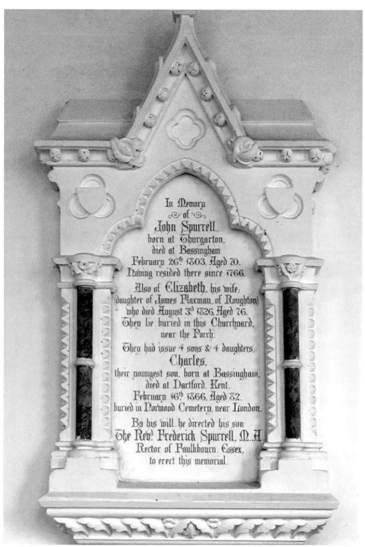

In Memory
of
John Spurrell,
born at Thurgarton,
died at Bessingham
February 26ᵗʰ 1803, Aged 70,
Having resided there since 1766.

Also of Elizabeth, his wife,
(daughter of James Flaxman, of Roughton)
who died August 3ʳᵈ 1826, Aged 76.
They lie buried in this Churchyard,
near the Porch.

They had issue 4 sons & 4 daughters.
Charles,
their youngest son, born at Bessingham,
died at Dartford, Kent,
February 16ᵗʰ 1866, Aged 52,
buried in Norwood Cemetery, near London.

By his will, he directed his son
The Revᵈ Frederick Spurrell, M.A.
Rector of Faulkbourn, Essex,
to erect this memorial.

Memorial to John and Elizabeth Spurrell in Bessingham
church, erected by their grandson the Rev. Frederick Spurrell
following the death of his father Charles.

There is a possibility that James is hinting at something in White Wig's private life that the family disapproved of – White Wig was a bachelor who lived most of his 79 years in the 1700s when morals were slightly looser than they became in the next century – but he also seems to be referring to the obstacles that had been placed before his brother William, who was expected to inherit the Thurgarton estate. In his will White Wig chose to overlook William's genetic right to be his heir, deciding instead to leave the estate in trust until William's son, William Dewing Spurrell, reached the age of 21, 'upon condition that the said William Spurrell my nephew shall within twelve calendar months next after my decease execute a legal conveyance of the land call'd Lords Lands lying intermixed with my lands in Bessingham and which was purchased by my late brother John Spurrell of Lord Viscount Anson'[25]. Although White Wig's nephews William and John went on to establish two distinct branches of the Spurrell family – one living at Thurgarton, the other at Bessingham – history almost took another course, and all because of the field known as Lords Lands. If the conveyance was not carried out, White Wig stipulated that the Thurgarton estate would be left to James instead. James, however, did not want to play his uncle's ridiculous posthumous games and create any more division in the family. An indenture dated 1808 states that William 'hath neglected to make such conveyance' but James, 'in consideration of the natural love and affection which he beareth towards his said brother'[26], decided to allow his brother and after him his nephew William Dewing Spurrell their rightful inheritance. It was agreed that a fine would be levied, known as a 'fine sur cognizance de droit come ceo qu'il a de son done', on two houses, 100 acres of arable land, 40 acres of pasture and 20 acres of meadow in Thurgarton, Bessingham, Gresham and Sustead. Once this was paid, James no longer had any claim on the estate and William finally began to manage it himself.

Estate management is rarely without problems, and the brief period of harmony in family relations was soon shattered when a dispute arose between William and his brother John. It was John who had inherited the Bessingham estate and he was also the surveyor of the roads in the village. The dispute, which flared up in 1816, concerned the use of the bridle lane and footpath that led from Bessingham, past Thurgarton House, to Sustead. John wanted to take his carts and carriages over it and had promised William that he would keep it in good repair. William, however, claimed that since John was not doing a good job keeping the public roads in good order it was unlikely that he would do the same for the lane past Thurgarton House. 'First let us see the man who does his duty well in a publick way, or there is but little prospect to think he will do it in a private one'[27], he wrote. Sections of the lane were apparently impassable on foot in the winter, and since William was not allowed to use tracks over John's land, he decided that, 'for the safety and quiet of myself and family as a prevention of dangers and unpleasant circumstances that might arise from being run down and over or annoyed by carts, wagons and carriages uncivil,' carts could only use the lane at his discretion. A concluding note says that unless John is willing to find a lawyer 'brassy enough' to pursue the case, there was nothing he could do about it.

~

More details about the family emerge in the letters of William's youngest sister, Frances, who in 1811 married a London coppersmith called Daniel Towers Shears. The Shears family owned a copper business in Southwark, supplying vats to Barclay Perkins & Co., the brewery where James and Charles worked. James had married Daniel's sister Rebecca in 1808 and six years later Charles would marry another of his sisters, Hannah. Unlike the aristocracy, the minor gentry were never ashamed of marrying into trade; and for merchants like Daniel, whose family had grown wealthy in the early days of the Industrial Revolution, they might appear less *nouveau riche* if joined in matrimony with a long-established family of landowners.

Frances's letters reveal her excitement and wonder at leaving rural Norfolk for the big city. 'I am much pleased with what I have seen of London'[28], she wrote on 28 May 1811. Her relatives in Norfolk sent her butter and hampers of turkey to remind her of the tastes of home. In 1815 Frances was told that she would have received crabs and lobsters from her mother at Cromer had it not been for the bad weather. There are references to gifts going in the other direction too. Frances's brother James sent a case of brown stout to his mother from the brewery on one occasion.

In 1812 Frances mentions a new house that her brother John was building at Bessingham. 'Give my kind love to him,' she told her sister Sarah, 'and tell him I wish him success in his undertaking and when finished to his mind may he live many, many years to enjoy it'[29]. The ruins of the old Manor House are located in a field south of the present Manor House, and in 2010 I was given permission by the landowner to explore them, but this reference in Frances's letter suggests there may have been two earlier houses on the site: one built in 1812 (which was later described as a 'neat mansion'[30]) and another in which the family had lived before that. Perhaps further archaeological work may one day uncover the truth.

A couple of years later, on 7 May 1814, John married his cousin Elizabeth Joy and at 5 o'clock in the morning exactly one year later their first child was born – a boy, whom John's mother described as 'a happy return of their wedding day'[31]. The boy was named Flaxman Spurrell in honour of his two grandmothers, Elizabeth and Mary, the daughters of James Flaxman.

Elizabeth, the paternal grandmother, had left Bessingham for Cromer after her husband's death. She lived in a house on Church Street and spent her final years sitting at the large bay window on the first floor, looking out towards Cromer church and the sea beyond, and enjoying her small garden to the rear*. She did not forget Bessingham, and when she died in 1826 she requested that fifty shillings of bread be distributed among the poor of the village.

Her sister Mary, the maternal grandmother of Flaxman Spurrell, was the aunt who had taken in the pregnant Mary Spurrell. She married Robert Joy, a miller who built two small windmills in Roughton. After his early death in 1794 Mary continued to run the mill and

---

* The house is now called Heath House after the chemist who occupied the ground floor for several decades after Elizabeth's death. The Spurrell family sold the property in the 1840s and it is now home to Lloyd's Pharmacy.

was later joined in partnership by her son Robert Bourne Joy. In 1814 they spent £5,000 replacing the small windmills with a 'very noble tower windmill, on a bold eminence, at the entrance of the village'[32].

Roughton Mill.

Many years later Robert allowed tourists to climb to the top of the windmill. A visitor to the area in 1841 recorded that Robert, 'with his usual urbanity, allows visitors to "tempt its giddy height" from which a wide expanse of the surrounding country may be seen'[33]. He also grew grapes and at a show held by the Holt Horticultural Society in 1834 his Frontignac grapes 'were generally praised, and obtained the first prize'[34]. Roughton Mill was later owned by the Spurrell family of Bessingham for a short period of time, as we shall see later on in Chapter 6.

Chapter 4

PROSPEROUS AND PICTURESQUE

In the eighteenth and nineteenth centuries Norfolk was considered the foremost county in terms of agricultural innovation and improvement. A combination of crop rotations (with the introduction of turnips and grasses), enclosure, soil amendments and long-term investment by enlightened and educated landowners had increased productivity on estates of all sizes. As the agriculturalist and politician Clare Sewell Read wrote in the 1890s, Norfolk 'was certainly the first county to adopt practical and theoretical improvements which have recently raised the pursuit of farming in the eyes of the world ... From the middle of the last century Norfolk has stood foremost in everything which tends to elevate this important branch of our national wealth'[35]. Pioneering figures such as 'Turnip' Townshend and Coke of Norfolk led the way on their vast estates, with smaller landowners following suit. The changes they introduced also gave us some of the features that make the North Norfolk countryside so pleasing to the eye: the picturesque hedge-lined fields, the large Georgian farmhouses surrounded by small parks and tall, majestic trees, and the large brick barns built as symbols of agricultural wealth. The landscape gardener Humphry Repton, who lived at Sustead Old

Hall from 1778 to 1786*, spoke of the area's 'enlightened character [which] helped to shape its reputation as a prosperous and picturesque part of the country'[36].

One indication of Bessingham's rising prosperity in the first half of the nineteenth century is the increase in the number of households from 19 to 31 between 1801 and 1841. Many of the new cottages were built by the Spurrells for estate workers – a sign that more and more labour was needed as the farming intensified. The population rose from 103 in 1801 to 139 in 1841 and remained roughly at this level for the rest of the century. During this period the Spurrells consolidated their position as the village's main landowners. By the 1830s most of the land in the village, as well as most of the cottages and the pub, belonged to the Bessingham estate.

~

When John Spurrell purchased his estate in 1766 he was described in some records as a maltster. Over the next few decades he and his son built up a business that grew barley, turned it into malt on the estate, and sold it to brewers as far away as London. Bryant's 1826 map of

---

* He later moved to Essex but the Reptons maintained close links with North Norfolk. Both Humphry's brother-in-law John Adey and his son William Repton were solicitors in Aylsham and William was also the steward for the Manor of Thurgarton with Bassingham. William represented the lord of the manor at manorial courts and oversaw admission to and surrender of copyhold land by tenants of the manor. He was probably instrumental in helping his brother George Stanley Repton acquire the lordship of the manor of Bessingham in the early 1800s.

Norfolk shows a malthouse next to the old Manor House. It was demolished in the nineteenth century but was probably a long, low building made of brick, with vents to control air flow and temperature. Malting was a seasonal activity that began after harvest time and provided employment in the winter months when farm work would otherwise be slow. It involved a number of stages to heat, cool, wet, dry and germinate the barley before the resulting malt was put into sacks and sent to the breweries. John's malt was shipped to London from Cromer and possibly down the Aylsham Navigation, which was completed in 1779, making the upper sections of the River Bure navigable. In the 1780s Norfolk malt (known as ship malt) began to replace West Country malt as the second largest source for London brewers after Hertfordshire. London's population was booming in the early days of the Industrial Revolution and all those extra people needed something to drink. Turning their barley into a commodity that could be purchased at London markets was a wise move by the two John Spurrells.

There was also a personal link. Robert Barclay and John Perkins had purchased the Anchor Brewery in Southwark in 1781. The writer and lexicographer Samuel Johnson famously said of the sale that 'we are not here to sell a parcel of boilers and vats, but the potentiality of growing rich beyond the dreams of avarice'[37]. Within a couple of decades Barclay Perkins & Co. was the largest brewery not just in London but in the world, exclusively producing porters and stouts. In 1790 Robert Barclay purchased Northrepps Hall and although he sold it to his brother-in-law Richard Gurney five years later, he had already established important links with local farmers and maltsters*. An article recently reproduced in *Brewery History* elaborates on the idea of a close personal link between Robert Barclay and his malt suppliers:

> This is evidently another feature of the change in ownership, for the Barclays and Gurneys were Norwich men, knowing the recent charges (sic) in the agriculture of East Anglia and the rising production of good barley on its sandy soils. It is not unlikely that there was a more specific connection; possibly through their own tenant farmers, or the farmer clients of the Norwich bankers. At all events, the brewery begins to receive supplies from Norfolk in 1781 and in the years afterwards takes active steps to develop the Norfolk market for malt, thus adding incentives for agricultural development[38].

As we saw in Chapter 3, both James and Charles Spurrell worked at Barclay Perkins & Co. in the early nineteenth century. In 1805 James wrote to his mother saying that 'John has nothing very serious to apprehend from his malting this year, his barley is not bought very dear'[39]. He told her that Norfolk malt was selling for 38 shillings per coomb† and Hertfordshire malt for 43 shillings at the time. James added the following

---

* The fascinating history of the intermarried Quaker clan of Gurneys, Barclays, Buxtons and Hoares is told by Verily Anderson in her two excellent books on the families (see Bibliography).
† A measurement equal to four bushels.

revealing postscript: 'Mr. Barclay frequently asks if I hear from you, and desires whenever I write, to give his respects to you, and my Uncle Flaxmans [James and William Flaxman]; he also speaks of the neatness of your house'[40]. There is no written evidence that the two John Spurrells supplied malt to Barclay Perkins & Co. (most of the brewery's early records went up in flames in 1832 although a few brewing books and other papers were 'gathered out of the ruins, arranged and bound by Chas. Spurrell after the Great Fire'[41]), but considering the fact that James and Charles Spurrell worked there and that Robert Barclay had visited their mother at Bessingham Manor House, I would conclude that it is almost certain that they did.

Because of the Great Fire at the brewery little information about James's and Charles's work has survived. In the 1820s Charles was experimenting with different ways of making porter and in 1834 James sought to determine how much salt had to be added to a pint of Thames water at 62 degrees Fahrenheit to make it the same weight as Ramsgate water. There is also a possible reference to one of them being the head brewer*.

---

* On 22 November 1840 *The Era* reported the death, 'after a short illness, of J. Spurrell, Esq., of Park-street, Southwark, in the 65th year of his age,' as well as that of 'Charles Spurrell, Esq., head brewer to the firm of Messrs. Barclay, Perkins, and Co.'[42]. Only James died that year, so the announcement of Charles's death is wrong and there is no way of knowing which of the brothers, in any, should have been referred to as the head brewer.

Charles, the youngest son of John Spurrell and Elizabeth Flaxman; he worked at Barclay Perkins & Co. in Southwark from 1813 to about 1840 before retiring to Dartford.

James and Charles lived on property belonging to the brewery, which was not uncommon for senior employees at the time. James lived for almost forty years on Park Street, opposite the entrance to the brewery. When he died in 1840 he was buried in the bishop's vault of Southwark cathedral (then St. Saviour's parish church), where a plaque in the nave of the cathedral was erected to his memory. Charles lived opposite James at 23 Park Street in the 1820s before moving to a much grander residence in Anchor Terrace on Southwark Bridge Road. All of these properties are still standing, and when 23 Park Street was sold by Southwark Council in 2013 it attracted the attention of the national press since it was the most expensive council house ever sold. After his brother's death Charles moved to Hill House in Dartford – a quieter and more salubrious location than industrial Southwark – and served as a magistrate and churchwarden for about twenty-five years*.

---

* The family's connections with the brewing trade did not end in 1840. Charles's son Frederick married his cousin Frances Gray, whose father John was a partner of the Gray & Dacre brewery in West Ham. Charles's niece Rebecca Spurrell married James Watney, who owned the Stag Brewery in Pimlico. After Watney's death in 1884 (leaving over £1 million) the firm became a private limited company and was the largest brewery in London. Its best known ale was Watney's Red Barrel, which was popular in the 1960s and 1970s.

Chapter 5

ENCLOSURE

On the morning of Monday, 20 May 1822 a meeting was held at the Horse Shoes Inn to discuss the enclosure of thirty acres of land in Bessingham that for centuries had served as common land. The enclosure was requested by John Spurrell and the other main landowners in the village and was the subject of an act of parliament entitled 'An Act for Inclosing Lands in the Parish of Bassingham in the County of Norfolk'. The common land was legally held by Viscount Anson as lord of the manor, but the right to use it belonged to everyone in the village. John Spurrell would have grazed his cattle on it, for example, as would the yeoman farmers, and for the many landless villagers it was also an important source of wood and furze for cooking and heating.

Common land held a special place in the collective consciousness: a place that belonged to nobody and to everybody at the same time. But to the new breed of capitalist farmer it was seen as unproductive waste land in need of 'improvement'. Although grazing was a common right, the common land was often overgrazed and enclosure was seen as a solution to this problem.

Enclosures had begun in the Tudor period, often by private agreement between farmers. In the Middle Ages the land in many villages was divided into large open fields and decisions were made at manorial courts about what would be grown in each field. Every villager would be allocated a certain number of strips in the fields and had to follow the communal planting plan. In the Tudor age East Anglian farmers began exchanging and combining their strips by mutual agreement, enclosing the larger areas they now owned with hedgerows, which had the added advantage of being able to contain grazing animals. Another benefit was that farmers could grow what they wanted and not what the manorial court told them to grow.

These early enclosures had few detractors but the new wave that took place from the 1760s to the 1820s was more controversial. Parliament was the driving force behind these new enclosures, recognising the economic benefits of increased production for the nation. But there were negative effects too. These so-called parliamentary enclosures were divisive in their day and historians continue to debate their impact on the countryside. Those on the left highlight the loss of long-held common rights and the eventual disappearance of the peasant and yeoman classes, who either became labourers or left the countryside to find new jobs in the cities; peasant smallholdings were absorbed by larger farms and labourers lived in tied cottages, which made them less secure. Historians on the right, however, point to the growth of production and wages, which benefited all of society, albeit disproportionately. The reality is probably somewhere in the middle and many historians today consider the enclosures to have been a necessary evil.

The Bessingham enclosure map, showing land ownership in the village in 1822 and calculations for the division of the common land.

~

Bessingham's common land was located in the south-west of the parish, either side of the road to Barningham and along the lane that leads to Manor Farm. The only modern clue to its existence is in the name of Common

Farm, which occupies some of the area that was once common land.

The Spurrell family were in a good position to benefit from the enclosure since the common land was divided according to the amount of land each landowner already possessed in the village. After inheriting the estate in 1803 John Spurrell had continued to expand it. He purchased mostly copyhold land from the Thaxter and England families (1807), his brother William (1811) and the Partridge family (1817), among others. Mary Partridge sold him fifteen acres of copyhold land for £430. In 1819 he bought the Horse Shoes Inn at auction in Norwich. It was being sold along with seven other pubs that were advertised as 'very desirable to brewers and publicans, and also to persons for investment of money, as they will all yield good rents'[43].

The act of parliament stated that the village contained 'certain commons and waste grounds containing thirty acres or thereabouts' of land of which Viscount Anson was lord of the manor and 'is or claims to be entitled to the soil of the said commons and waste grounds,' and that John Spurrell and others owned land in the village, and the:

> commons and waste grounds, in their present state, yield very little profit to the several persons interested therein; and it would be advantageous to the several persons interested in the said commons and waste grounds, if the rights of common in, over, and upon the same were extinguished, and if the said commons and waste grounds were

divided and inclosed, and specific parts or shares thereof allotted to the several persons interested therein, according to their several and respective estates, rights, and interests, in, over or upon the same[44].

The act was passed and most of the common land was allocated to John Spurrell. The other beneficiaries were Philip Wynell Mayow of Hanworth Hall, Lord Suffield of Gunton Hall, William Windham of Felbrigg Hall, Snelling Roper of Thurgarton, and John Butterfield, Timothy Puxley and James Brooke of Bessingham. Within a few decades the smallholdings of Butterfield, Puxley and Brooke had been absorbed by the Bessingham estate or the even larger Felbrigg estate. In 1837 John Butterfield's widow Susanna sold their cottage and land, including a garden 'well planted with choice fruit-trees in full bearing'[45], to John Spurrell. By the 1850s the Puxleys' property had become part of the Felbrigg estate and Francis Puxley was receiving poor relief. Of all the early nineteenth century yeoman families only the Franklands survived. They had occupied what is now Manor House Farm in the 1700s and Manor Farm in the 1800s and 1900s. Although they were not awarded any common land, they did own Church Cottages and were very involved in village life for several generations.

~

A drawing of Bessingham church in about 1820 by Robert Ladbrooke shows several cracks in the walls. About 40 years later it was considered to have 'fallen into complete decay and ... no longer fit for the decent celebration of Divine Service[46]. Many churches in the early nineteenth century had been neglected in this way. The neglect was not only structural but spiritual too. Bessingham was one of many parishes around the country with an absentee clergyman. The Rev. Isaac Avarne was appointed Rector of Bessingham in 1772 and held the position until his death in 1820. But in 1786 he also became Rector of Halesworth in Suffolk and it was there that he lived, leaving the work of caring for the souls of Bessingham to a curate, who was paid a stipend from the tithes. William Repton, the Aylsham solicitor who had spent some of his childhood at Sustead, handled Avarne's accounts, collecting tithes as well as the rent for the parsonage, and paying for repairs and other expenses. In 1807 the 'parsonage, house, barn, outbuildings and glebe land'[47] were let to Joshua Denney for £35, which was payable half yearly at Lady Day and Michaelmas.

Bessingham church by Robert Ladbrooke, c. 1820.

Avarne was described as 'a man of strong sense, and the strictest integrity; of warm and generous feelings, and a most sincere and steady friend'[48]. He died at Halesworth in 1820 at the age of 80 and there is no indication that he was on bad terms with the Bessingham inhabitants despite the fact that they had to pay tithes to an absent rector. His successor, the Rev. William Walker, got off to a rough start, though. He wrote to Repton from Stuston in Suffolk on 11 September 1820 to introduce himself. Having been presented by Lord Anson, 'it is natural, you know, for a fresh incumbent to make enquiries after the state of his preferment'[49]. Following the enclosure of the common land he became embroiled in a dispute with John Spurrell. Walker had calculated John's annual tithes to be £45 but John refused to pay more than £38. 'I have told him I have no doubt you will be displeased with the line of conduct he adopts'[50], Repton explained to Walker. On Boxing Day 1823 he wrote of Spurrell's 'unhandsome and unexpected' behaviour, which is 'undeserved, and not at all answerable to the candour which I have always shewn him'[51]. In January 1824 John, realising that he had not taken into account the additional land he had been awarded under the enclosure act and accepting that the error was entirely his own, went to see Repton, being 'so much vexed' and protesting that 'he had no intention to deceive you in his conference with you'[52]. He agreed to pay £6 0s 6d on top of the £38 he was already giving Walker. John was not the only parishioner giving Walker a headache that year. William Spurrell and Snelling Roper were late in their payments and Repton insisted that the parishioners 'seem somewhat tardy but they must be brought into better order'[53].

In December 1824 Walker wrote to Repton regarding a rise in the price of 'all corns,' which would result in higher tithes. However, 'what to say of Mr. J. Spurrell, I know not, wishing sincerely to be upon the best terms with him'[54]. Walker said he hoped to receive an additional sixpence per acre for grassland. 'I shall be content, for I love peace: but you will be so good as to manage with him as well as you can'[55]. He also used the opportunity to ask Repton to remind parishioners once again to pay on time, but the request fell on deaf ears. In a letter dated 28 January 1825 he reported that William Spurrell and William Bacon were taking a 'very unreasonable' time to pay, adding that they 'seem to treat me in an unhandsome manner,' especially Spurrell. Walker apologised to Repton for the Bessingham parishioners, lamenting that they 'occasion unnecessary trouble for you and do not, probably, on account of distance, appear to use much ceremony with me'[56].

Tithes had traditionally been paid to the clergy in kind but in most parishes these had been replaced by monetary payments by the early nineteenth century. In 1836 the Tithe Commutation Act formalised this change and on 1 June 1838 Daniel Spurrell and William Dewing Spurrell, landowners 'whose interest is not less than one-fourth of the whole value of lands subject to tithes'[57] in Bessingham, called a parish meeting at the Horse Shoes Inn to discuss the matter. The change in the amounts is insignificant but tithe maps were drawn for each parish and are now a valuable resource for local historians (see page 82).

PART THREE

1840 ~ 1890

Chapter 6

KIND-HEARTED AND SINCERE

The Queen's diamond jubilee in 1897 was also used as an occasion for the people of Bessingham to reflect on Daniel Spurrell's sixty years as their squire. A special service was held at the church to mark the royal jubilee, followed by dinner and an afternoon of sports, dancing and fireworks at the Manor House. It was a 'decided success,' noted the parish magazine. 'It was a day too which will long be remembered by the people of Bessingham: it afforded further proof, if such were needed, of the kind-hearted interest, and sincere regard, our squire has for the welfare of all his people'[58].

Daniel was the second son of John Spurrell and Elizabeth Joy and was most probably named after his uncle, Daniel Towers Shears*. He was sent away to school where he learned the skills expected of a gentleman farmer. I have not been able to find the name of the school in any family papers or archives, but it may well have been the Pottergate Street Academy in Norwich, which his Thurgarton cousins also attended at this time (see Chapter 8). In an undated letter to his

---

* It is also likely that Daniel Towers Shears was his godfather, since it was not uncommon at the time for children to be named after their godparents.

mother, Daniel asks her to forward his English grammar book as well as his sister Betsy's French grammar book if she could find it at home. He also asks for a leather bottle, 'which if you will fill with something good I shall feel obliged'[59]. I know of only two examples of his school work that have survived. One is a remarkably accurate map of Africa, which he drew in 1831. Map making and map reading were useful skills for landowners and his cousin Richard, who studied at the Academy at the same time, produced several maps – some better than others – of Norfolk, England, Italy, Europe, Africa and Asia. Daniel's other surviving work is a copy of a poem entitled 'Piety', written in neat copperplate handwriting and decorated with elaborate ink outlines of swans and a fish. It is signed 'Daniel Spurrell – Scripsit 1830' and concludes with a note on the importance of a good education:

Nothing is so universally advantageous to mankind or ornamental to human nature as an accomplished and virtuous education.

Although Daniel was his father's second son, it was he rather than his elder brother Flaxman who inherited the Bessingham estate. Flaxman had chosen to pursue a career in medicine instead but he was given a small parcel of land in Bessingham as well as the Sidestrand estate that his father had purchased from James Flaxman in 1811. Flaxman studied at the Webb Street School of Anatomy and Medicine in Southwark and later at Guy's and St. Thomas's Hospital. He qualified as a surgeon in 1838 and practiced first at Mile End, London, in partnership with Thomas Allen, 'surgeons, apothecaries and accoucheurs'[60], before settling in Bexleyheath, Kent.

A keen amateur archaeologist, he had collected fossils on the Cromer cliffs as a boy and went on to be a founding member of the Kent Archaeological Society and president of the West Kent Natural History, Microscopical and Photographic Society.

Some of Daniel's correspondence with Flaxman in the years after their father's death has been preserved on microfilm at the Norfolk Record Office, giving us an insight into the life of the young squire as he went about modernising his estate and taking on various roles in society. He also kept Flaxman informed of family events that were taking place in Norfolk. On New Year's Day 1840 their grandmother Mary Joy celebrated her birthday. 'Mother and Elizabeth and Fanny are just gone [to Roughton] to dine and drink her health. I think she is in her 86th year but am not certain'[61]. Flaxman's replies have not survived, but apparently he was using language that some family members were having trouble understanding. Daniel told him in 1840 that he should send their aunt Sarah Joy a dictionary 'as she cannot find some of your words in the one she has got'[62]. In the spring of 1840 Daniel had a 'very pleasant'[62] dinner with a party of gentlemen, hosted by his cousin William Dewing Spurrell at Thurgarton House, and in September of the following year he wrote of plans to shoot at Sidestrand with Richard James Spurrell and Robert Ives, hoping to send some game to his relatives in London afterwards.

Occasionally Daniel vented his anger at something that annoyed him, such as the wedding of Queen Victoria to Prince Albert on 10 February 1840. 'This memorable day I for my part can see no reason to rejoice in. It will pass over with little notice from me,' he wrote, giving it quite considerable notice nevertheless: 'Who is Prince Albert? A man of no power, no property – a nobody. Such an alliance can be of no service to the British nation – a mere love match – our Queen be ever happy in her choice'[63]. Ironically, not only would Prince Albert mostly likely have been very pleased with the way in which Daniel cultivated his image as a benevolent and enlightened squire, but there is also a photograph of Daniel in which he bears a passing resemblance to the Prince Consort. Daniel was enraged by something else that day too. Having been asked by his solicitor to sign some papers he felt he had no reason to sign, he concluded: 'I am not satisfied – I might as well turn Roman Catholic at once'[64].

Daniel Spurrell (left) and his brother Flaxman Spurrell (right). Daniel could almost pass as Prince Albert in this photograph.

Another matter that annoyed Daniel was the unsystematic way in which Flaxman was answering his letters. On 19 January 1841 he wrote: 'Now it comes to my turn to war with you about not answering my letters in proper order but I do not intend to make much ado but merely to remind you that people who hold out the importance of answering letters daily should be careful to practice what they preach lest they cause an alarm heedlessly'[65]. The collection of letters comes to an abrupt end shortly after that.

~

Brighton was a fashionable seaside resort in the nineteenth century and it was here that Daniel Spurrell and Sarah Frances Copeman chose to marry despite both being from Norfolk. On 11 May 1848 the ceremony was held at St. Nicholas's Church, with Daniel's cousin Frederick, then the curate of nearby Newhaven, officiating. Sarah was the youngest daughter of Robert and Blanche Copeman of Itteringham House (now White House Farm). She was one of thirteen children and her eldest brother, Edward James Copeman, had married Daniel's aunt, Mary Joy, in 1833. Daniel and Sarah had probably known each other for some time before their engagement. Within ten and a half years of their wedding day Sarah had given birth to seven children: Emily Fanny (1849), Blanche Elizabeth (1850), Katherine Anne (1852), Sarah Maria (1854), Robert John (1855), Mary Isabelle (1857) and Edmund Denham (1858). Of the seven only Sarah failed to survive infancy, dying at the age of nine months after suffering 'teething convulsions'[66]. Her small stone cross lies among the family graves near the porch of Bessingham church. As the family grew, Daniel and Sarah employed a governess to assist with their children's education. For example, Annie Hays, a governess born in Kent, was living at the Manor House in 1861. Robert and Denham were later sent away to boarding school (see Chapter 8). The rigid class structure of the nineteenth century meant that Daniel's children would have lived quite separate lives from the other boys and girls in the village and they would have looked forward immensely to visits from distant relatives or other gentry families.

Daniel and Sarah Frances Spurrell in an unusually informal pose for the nineteenth century.

The Rev. Frederick Spurrell (centre) with his wife, children, servants and quite a few animals by the tennis court in front of Faulkbourne Rectory, Essex, in 1882. They are joined by Daniel Spurrell's children; Denham is second from the right, next to my great-grandfather Charles.

Daniel remained close to his cousin Frederick and in 1872 Frederick's son Charles (my great-grandfather) came to stay at Bessingham Manor House during his school holidays. Charles was besotted with Daniel's youngest daughter, Mary, and he sent her a letter not long after returning to Felsted School. Mary wrote back on 10 August: 'I was not astonished at your writing so soon, but, was only very glad to find you were such a good little boy as to keep your promise, and I hope that you will continue in the same good way as you have begun with, as I shall be always very pleased to receive your letters'; she ended 'with very best love as you see from my [pink] paper'[67]. On 21 August she wrote again, thanking Charles for the long letter she had received in the meantime, 'but I want it still to be longer as I shall always have much delight in reading your letters'[68]. She wrote about a croquet party that she and her sister Emily had attended, stoking his jealousy by saying she had danced with 'such a nice boy, he was dark and about sixteen years of age. His name I had better not mention I think'. She concluded: 'I hope that you will write to me soon as I want a letter most dreadfully'[69].

Six days later she wrote again to wish Charles a happy birthday. 'You do not know what a lot of good wishes I have for you, they would take more than a hundred of these sheets to fill, so I think that you must be satisfied with only hearing a few of them'[70]. She then referred to the boy she had danced with earlier in the month. She was not pleased with Charles's response, although she knew very well that he would not be happy. 'I did not say that you would be afraid of the boy I danced with nor did I wish you to be. What made you think it was H. Brown? I did not know that you know him even but as it happens it was not. It was Shepherd Hartley. H. B. has not been to stay with us, but Mama, Papa and Robert went to stay at Mr. Brown's a week but Harry is at School'. She scolded Charles for taking 'such a liberty' of calling her Pops. She told him to find another nickname 'if it is a pretty one but otherwise stick to Mary'[71]. On 4 September she sent her fourth and final letter, 'as my sisters do not think it is proper that I should keep up a regular correspondence'[72]. Perhaps regretting the tone she had taken in her previous letter, she asked for one more from Charles 'and please let it be a long one as it is the last'. In case her request was unclear, she added a postscript: 'Please not to forget the letter and let it be the longest you have sent me'[73].

The Rev. Frederick Spurrell (left) and his son the Rev. Charles Henry Spurrell (right).

I have only five letters that belonged to Charles, my great-grandfather. A few years after these letters were written he followed in his father's footsteps by going up to Corpus Christi College, Cambridge, to study Holy Orders. Later he spent about fifteen years travelling the country, preaching on behalf of the National Society and raising funds for new schools. He must have received thousands of letters in his lifetime, professionally as well as privately. He lost both a fiancée and a wife but none of the letters of condolence have survived. For some reason the five letters that still exist include the four he received in the summer of 1872 from his cousin Mary.

She had played with his teenage emotions and maybe he wanted to keep the letters as a memento of an infatuation that never faded*.

John Tuck outside the old Manor House whilst employed as a groom. The occupants of the trap are unknown.

In one of the letters Mary mentioned taking 'John and Charley Tuck and little George and Susan' for lessons every morning[74]. John and Charley Tuck had lost their father in 1865 and their mother in 1868 when she and two of her other children were killed after a cart overturned on a lane in Thurgarton. Aged nine and six respectively,

---

* The other letter, from his time as curate of Banbury in the 1890s, was from a parishioner who claimed he had 'that rare gift supposed to belong exclusively to the highest type of Romish priests, very difficult to describe, but which makes one feel that you could be spoken to with perfect ease on any possible subject'[75].

John and Charley were orphaned and faced the prospect of spending the rest of their childhoods in the workhouse. The kindest and perhaps most heart-warming act in Daniel's life was to provide John and Charley with a room at the Manor House. He ensured that they were given some schooling and later employed them on the estate. For somebody like Daniel, with a strong sense of Victorian duty and paternalism, it was his moral obligation to provide work for the poor as the best way of alleviating their hunger and suffering. The welfare state was still a long way off and as an employer he not only gave work to people in the village but also satisfied his social conscience. He saw himself as a One Nation Tory*. As a guardian on the board of the Erpingham Poor Law Union since 1838 Daniel was probably all too aware of the appalling conditions in Victorian workhouses and the harsh treatment that inmates received. It is perhaps a testament to his concern for his tenants' welfare that the census records for West Beckham workhouse between 1851 and 1901 list no inmates who were born in Bessingham, even though the surrounding villages of Thurgarton, Gresham and

---

* Indeed, in 1878 he took the trouble of copying down a quote by Disraeli, the champion of One Nation conservativism, in his farm account book: 'What the Earl of Beaconsfield said!! Mr. Gladstone was a sophistical rhetorician inebriated with the exuberance of his own verbosity and gifted with an egotistical imagination that can at all times commend an interminable and inconsistent series of arguments to malign his opponents and to glorify himself'[76].

Sustead sent several paupers to the workhouse during this time*.

John Tuck spent all of his 94 years in Bessingham, working as a groom or coachman, as a personal attendant to Denham Spurrell, and with the other men in the fields or in the gardens of the Manor House. He will crop up again several times throughout the book. His brother Charley, however, left Bessingham in the 1870s to work as a footman to Sir Henry Josiah Stracey at Rackheath Hall, and I have found no record of him after 1881.

~

In the 1860s Daniel inherited substantial amounts of money from his mother, aunt and uncle that enabled him to build a new Manor House, purchase additional land and fund the restoration of the village church.

In 1863 his debonair uncle Robert Bourne Joy, the owner of Roughton Mill, passed away. As with the Flaxman property in previous generations, the Joy possessions would eventually come into Daniel's hands. Robert left a personal estate that was originally calculated to be worth about £8,000. This included not only the mill and 70 acres of farmland in Roughton and Felbrigg but also 380 acres in Billockby, on the Norfolk Broads, where he was also lord of the manor; he left all of this to his sister Sarah. He bequeathed legacies to his friends, including £200 to Frances Peele Bayfield and £2,000 to be

---

* The only Bessingham-born inmate I have found is Charlotte Bumfrey, the former village postwoman, who is recorded as living at the workhouse in 1911 at the age of 87 – she died in 1914 at the age of 89.

held in trust for the benefit of Frances and her two children, Frederick and Caroline. Frederick also received £1,000 for his own benefit. The obvious conclusion to be made from these generous bequests is that Robert was Frederick and Caroline's father, especially considering that Frederick's middle name was Robert.

Frances Bayfield was born in Cromer in 1808 and gave birth to Frederick in 1832 and Caroline in 1836. They were christened at Thwaite and their father's name was left blank in the parish register. In 1841 Frederick was at school in Roughton and we can only assume that his school fees were being paid by Robert. He later moved to Taunton, where he worked as a brewery clerk, but his sister remained in Norfolk and married Edwin Denney, a chemist in North Walsham whose grandfather Joshua had been Isaac Avarne's tenant at Glebe Farm in Bessingham in the early 1800s. Significantly, Frances, who outlived Robert by three years, was buried at Roughton.

Robert was also a remarkably good artist and several of his works have survived, including two painted doors that once hung inside the mill house in Roughton and are now at the Gressenhall Farm and Workhouse museum. He painted portraits of family members, including his mother, sister Elizabeth and cousin Charles Spurrell. He also had links with the Norwich School of Artists, and a portrait of him by George Clint was sold at auction in 1930[*].

---

[*] I have black-and-white photographs of many of these family portraits but since the original paintings were sold and I cannot trace the present owners I am unable to publish them in this book without infringing upon copyright laws.

Robert's sister Elizabeth (Daniel's mother) died at Sidestrand Lodge in 1866. She divided her household possessions between her two sons – the china marked S going to Daniel and the china marked F to Flaxman, for example – and set aside £1,000 to be used for the 'maintenance and benefit'[77] of their sister Betsy, who had been placed in a lunatic asylum in Norwich. Flaxman inherited Sidestrand Lodge but sold it to Samuel Hoare* fourteen years later for £8,000[78].

Robert's last surviving sister, Sarah, lived at the mill until her death in 1867, when she died with a personal estate calculated to be worth £8,000. She left property in Roughton, Felbrigg, Cromer and Overstrand to Daniel, and the Billockby estate to Daniel and Flaxman jointly. She also left £500 for the benefit of her servants, with the interest being for their own use and not their husbands'.

On 15 May 1867, four days before Sarah died, Daniel had attended an auction at the White Horse Inn, Great Yarmouth, for 88 acres of land in Billockby and Burgh St. Margaret. On his copy of the auction programme he recorded the bids. For Lot 1 (70 acres) his original bid was for £3,500 but he was forced to go up to £4,250, plus £98 10s for the timber growing on the land. He did not bid on the other lots. He paid a deposit of £637 10s on the day of the auction and the balance five months later. In September 1868 he leased the 70 acres and a farmhouse to George Manship for £150 per annum, retaining the game rights for himself. Daniel later bought his brother's interest in the 380 acres of land in Billockby that had been left to them by their Aunt Sarah. He also became lord of

---

* Hoare was a Norwich M. P. from 1886 to 1906 and became a baronet in 1899.

the manor of Billockby, adding it to the title of lord of the manor of Bessingham that he had acquired in 1867*.

Daniel was now the owner of Roughton Mill but he chose not to keep it. In 1867 he placed an advertisement in *The Norfolk Chronicle*, stating that the mill contained 'three pairs of stones, with patent sails, seven floors and capable of grinding on an average six lasts of corn'[79]. The property also included a house and four acres of pasture, all freehold. Daniel was asking £4,500 for this and fifteen acres of farmland in Cromer and Overstrand. In June 1868 he was approached by Benjamin Bond Cabbell of Cromer Hall, who offered him £3,500. They eventually settled on a price of £3,750 and in October of that year Daniel held an auction to sell some of the items at the mill that neither he nor Bond Cabbell wanted, including draught horses, riding horses, carts, harnesses, three hundred books, a mangle and a hay engine. The following month Daniel's nephew Frank Brown signed a lease with Bond Cabbell to begin occupying the house and operating the windmill at Christmas. Frank's father James had run the mill at Itteringham and married one of the daughters of Robert Copeman. In the 1880s the Press family took over Roughton Mill and it stayed in operation until 1906 when a strong gale forced the sails to turn backwards. It caught light as a result of the tremendous amount of heat created by the friction. It remained derelict until 1978, when work began to turn it into the headquarters of the local scout group.

---

* On the death of George Stanley Repton in 1858 the lordship of the manor of Bessingham had passed to the Aylsham solicitor William Henry Scott, who sold it to Daniel.

Although he sold the mill, Daniel kept Flaxman's Farm in Roughton and leased it. In 1869 John Clark agreed to rent it for eight years at £190 per annum.

Daniel therefore inherited large amounts of money and land in the 1860s. In 1873 the *Return of Owners of Land in England and Wales*, the most comprehensive survey of land ownership in Britain since Domesday Book, showed that he owned 774 acres in Norfolk (mostly in Bessingham, Roughton and Billockby) with an annual rent value of £1,377 13s. But the story of the Joy inheritance took a further twist after the death of his parents' cousin Mary Anne Cann in 1882. Mary Anne was the only child of William Flaxman and had married the Rev. John Stephenson Cann of Wramplingham Hall, near Wymondham. In January 1883 Daniel signed an affidavit stating in rather complex legal terms that since Mary Anne had died childless, her father's sisters Elizabeth and Mary became entitled to one moiety each of the residue of William Flaxman's estate 'in reversion expectant'[80] on the death of Mary Anne. Elizabeth and Mary were long deceased and their moieties therefore passed down to their heirs. Elizabeth's share went to her many grandchildren, but Mary's was traced through her heirs – her son Robert, then her daughter Sarah – to Daniel. Robert's personal estate at the time of his death was recalculated to about £12,000 and Sarah's to £16,000, and in 1883 Daniel very unexpectedly received a large windfall of £6,353 14s 3d.

~

On 27 March 1867 the Rector of Bessingham, the Rev. Henry Charrington Fisher, wrote to Daniel enclosing his annual rent for the glebe land and a circular he had printed at Daniel's suggestion:

Bassingham Church, Norfolk

This church having fallen into complete decay and being no longer fit for the decent celebration of Divine Service, an effort is being made to restore it. The cost of its restoration, £450, is a sum quite beyond the power of the parish, a very poor and small one, to meet.

All therefore who would aid in rescuing God's House from ruin, and in enabling a poor parish to worship Him decently and in order, are earnestly invited to assist the Incumbent in his undertaking to raise a fund for these objects.

Subscriptions will be most thankfully received by the Rector,

REV. H. C. FISHER

BASSINGHAM,

NEAR HANWORTH[81].

Underneath were written in pen the words 'or by Daniel Spurrell Esqr., Bassingham Hall'. Two months later Sarah Joy died and Daniel decided to contribute several hundred pounds of the money he inherited from her to the church restoration fund. The church was important to him personally. He was keenly aware of his duty in the village and felt that it was his moral obligation to lead by example by attending church services, 'an example all the more valuable as it was very rare in that

71

neighbourhood for a man in his position to be so particular in the matter of public worship[182]. The timing of the restoration is also significant because the Rev. H. C. Fisher was perhaps the first Rector of Bessingham in almost a century who took his role seriously. He and Daniel joined forces to push through the long overdue restoration of Bessingham church. Their application for a grant from the Diocese of Norwich was turned down.

Routine repairs are mentioned in church records in the 1700s and early 1800s, including work on the belfry in 1855, but nothing on the scale of the 1869 restoration had been carried out for centuries. William Chapman, a builder from Hanworth, was commissioned to do the work and in the job specifications he explained the various steps. The preliminary tasks involved removing the roof tiles and unsafe parts of the south wall and taking up the flooring, carefully ensuring that gravestones, brasses and memorials were preserved. The floor was excavated to a depth of nine inches and filled with six inches of concrete. The south wall was then rebuilt with additional buttresses and the north wall was smoothed out in preparation for the new roof. The old plaster was replaced with stucco, and Staffordshire tiles were laid in the nave and Minton tiles in the chancel. The carpenter and joiner then used oak timber 'of English growth, straight grained and well seasoned'[183] for the new benches, pulpit and altar rail. The benches replaced the old box pews that had probably been installed after the Reformation, and the pulpit was moved to the north wall. The last step was to install the new roof and gutters.

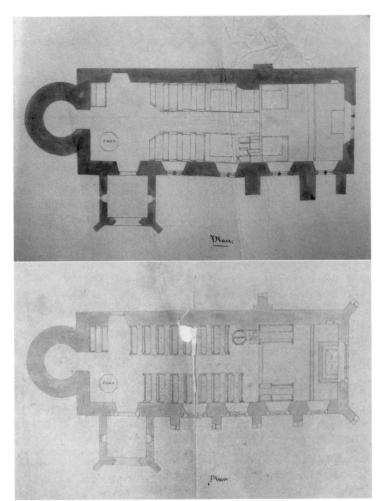

Plans of Bessingham church before (top) and after (bottom) the 1869 restoration. The box pews in the nave and chancel were removed and the pulpit was placed against the north wall; buttresses were added to support the exterior walls.

The church reopened on 17 November and three services were held that day to mark the occasion. The Dean of Norwich preached at Holy Communion in the early morning and at 11.30 Morning Prayer was led by a number of local clergy, including the incumbents of Bessingham, Aldborough, Gresham, Gimingham and Roughton. An evening service was held at 3.30 and attended by the Rural Dean of Repps.

The choir and harmonium 'contributed to the solemnity and heartiness of the services,' and the collections throughout the day, which amounted to £33, 'enabled the church to be declared free from all debt'[84]. A number of items were offered as decorations, including 'a very beautiful and costly altar cloth' made by Daniel's wife Sarah and 'a handsome kneeling cushion for the communion rail, worked in wools by the Misses Spurrell'[85].

The restoration was not only necessary to prevent the building from eventually becoming derelict, but for the parson and squire it reasserted the church's position as the driving moral force in the village. For decades the poor had been drifting away from the Established Church. Between 1831 and 1871 four thousand Nonconformist chapels were built across the country, including a Methodist chapel in Bessingham, which held services until the mid-1900s. In the 1880s Thomas Cooper, a labourer on the Bessingham estate, preached there and, like many Methodists, was also closely associated with the trade union movement, serving as a local branch officer[86].

The squire and the parson were not always steadfast allies, though, and Daniel did not see eye to eye with Fisher's successor, the Rev. Skeffington Armstrong. In a letter sent to him on 6 September 1872 from Barningham Rectory (probably from the Rev. James Wilson), marked 'private,' the writer alludes to a misunderstanding with Armstrong. He told Daniel not to get too worked up and suggested 'pity and prayers' rather than enmity regarding Armstrong's behaviour. He tactfully added that if Daniel wished to avoid Armstrong at church that week, it was 'our Communion Sunday at Barningham'[87].

~

Daniel's most iconic contribution to the landscape of Bessingham, one that reflected the confidence of the mid-Victorian gentry, was the new Manor House he built in 1870. He made the bold move of turning one of the roads in the village into the driveway to the house and building a replacement road. Called New Road, it lies to the north of Manor House Farm, but the original route to the south of the farmhouse can still be seen by tracing field boundaries. The relocation of the road explains why the farmhouse now appears to face away from the road.

The plans for the new Manor House were drawn up by Thomas Lawrie, a London architect, and Daniel signed an agreement with the builder William Chapman on 20 November 1869, just three days after the doors of Bessingham church were opened to reveal Chapman's work there. Chapman had carried out work for Daniel as early as 1855, when he demolished and rebuilt a pair of cottages in Roughton for £425.

The Manor House was built entirely of brick, with three floors above a vaulted cellar. The large sitting and drawing rooms were off the entrance hall and had wide south-facing bay windows that overlooked the parkland

and the site of the earlier manor house* and farm buildings. On the other side of the hall was the study, which could also be accessed from the servants' passage that led down the centre of the house to the yard outside. This allowed tenants and tradesmen to reach Daniel's study without having to use the main entrance. A range of rooms typical of a Victorian manor house are found on each side of the servants' passage, including the kitchen, scullery, larder, pantry and laundry room. There was also a back staircase leading to the first floor. Outside the courtyard door were the dairy, washhouse, game larder, coal house, knife room and gun room. There was also a WC on the ground floor, which could only be accessed from the outside. On the first floor there were seven bedrooms in the main house and one above the washroom, which was accessed from the yard – this was no doubt the room in which John and Charley Tuck slept in the early 1870s. There was also a bathroom, two dressing rooms and a housemaids' closet, and stairs leading up to the four servants' bedrooms in the attic.

Though attractive and situated in a prominent location, the house is not considered architecturally spectacular, despite a handful of interesting features. Nikolaus Pevsner ignored it in his comprehensive survey of the buildings of Norfolk, and in a book on country houses by John Kenworthy-Browne, Bessingham Manor House is described as a 'not very large, red-brick Victorian house, with Dutch gables and brick quoins'[88]. The gables are indeed worth mentioning, and along with the chimneys they give the impression that the house is reaching upwards, sitting tall and proud.

---

* Or houses (see page 34).

Bessingham Manor House photographed (above) c. 1880 (the two gentlemen in the foreground are probably Daniel Spurrell, facing the house, and Denham Spurrell, facing the camera) and sketched (below) in 1893 by the Rev. R. J. Simpson, Rector of Metton and Felbrigg.

Another feature of interest is the covered porch, or porte-cochère, which collapsed in the mid-1900s. It allowed people to step in and out of their carts or carriages without getting wet, and was still in use in the 1930s when my grandparents parked their car underneath it.

To do it justice the new Manor House needed to be surrounded by a 'polite' landscape, and so Daniel set about designing the parkland, woodland, grotto and walled garden. Several fields were converted into parkland and sown with grass so that it could be grazed by sheep*. It was separated from the house by a brick and flint ha-ha. The area between the old and new roads was converted into a walled garden, which grew fruits, vegetables and flowers for the house. A wall was built along New Road from the farm buildings to the entrance of the driveway, where a tower, or dovecote, was erected in 1874 to designs by Daniel's nephew, the architect Herbert Spurrell[†]. It was described in the following terms: 'its upper half has half-timber work with herring-bone brick nogging and is octagonal in shape. The latter form is maintained in the rather high-pitched roof, which has tiny dormers through which the pigeons emerge. A small weather-vane crowns the top of the roof'[89].

---

* Black sheep grazed the parkland in the mid-twentieth century.

† Having trained under Alfred Waterhouse, Herbert practised for many years in Eastbourne, where he designed churches, schools and residential buildings. The tower in Bessingham was one of his first projects.

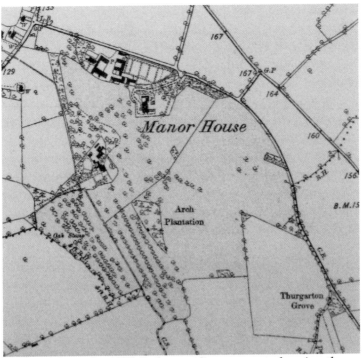

Detail from the 1885 Ordnance Survey map, showing the
Manor House, parkland and walled garden. The old manor
house and farm buildings are also visible; a line of trees to the
east of the old house and a field boundary indicate the route
of the former driveway (see also map, p. 82). The old road to
the south of Manor House Farm can be traced along a field
boundary to its junction with The Street.

Around the house and along the driveway trees and
shrubs were planted, including saplings that John Mott
of Barningham Hall had given Daniel in November 1871.
These included an Austrian pine, Corsican pine, Douglas
fir, noble fir, Nordmann fir, Morinda spruce and
Wellingtonea gigantea (or giant sequoia, the first

79

specimens of which had arrived in Britain in the 1850s). The gardens also contained a mediaeval church font, which had been presented to Daniel by the Rev. C. J. Lucas, Rector of Burgh St. Margaret, after the church acquired a new font. It was still in the gardens in the 1930s but has since disappeared. A grotto was also erected in the walled garden, built of bricks and stones collected from a number of sources.

The new Manor House was not simply for living in. Its large reception rooms, each about 18 by 23 feet, were ideal for dinner parties and entertaining. Marion Philpott, whose father was Rector of Thwaite in the 1880s and 1890s, considered the Spurrells 'very great friends'*. She later recalled that 'these friendly people were constantly entertaining and I remember my first parties there very vividly'[90]. Sadly no photographs have survived of the interior of the house at this time, although it is known that portraits of Daniel and Sarah and their children hung on the wall of the staircase from the 1880s onwards. The Anglo-American artist James Jebusa Shannon was commissioned to paint the family and in 1883 he exhibited his portrait of Daniel's daughter Katherine (Kitty) at the Royal Academy. Most of these portraits were sold in the twentieth century and their current whereabouts are unknown. Daniel and Sarah's portraits were auctioned at Sotheby's in 1974, for example, but the paintings of their children Emily and Denham still belong to different branches of the family.

---

* Marion later married Robert Ives of Erpingham House; her sister Ada married Dr. William Spurrell of Aldborough and her sister Violet married John Spurrell of Newton St. Faith.

Chapter 7

THE APPEARANCE OF PLENTY

Farming was at its peak in Norfolk in the middle of the nineteenth century. It was characterised by high levels of capital investment and production and the widespread use of marl and manure to improve soil fertility. It was known to contemporaries as a period of High Farming. In 1843 an advertisement for the sale of the Thurgarton Hall estate, which contained 300 acres of land in Thurgarton and Bessingham, said that it was in a 'highly respectable part of the county, and surrounded by the seats of resident nobility and gentry,' with easy access to the 'fashionable bathing town of Cromer' and various market towns. The advertisement also mentioned the 'salubrity of the air,' and the 'superior quality of the land'[91].

In Bessingham, soon after inheriting his father's estate, Daniel set about modernising and improving it. By 1840 he had demolished the old malthouse and other outbuildings and begun work on new structures, including a granary. The malt tax had been increasing steadily and eating into the profits of maltsters. 1840 turned out to be a bad year for barley, and Daniel was no doubt satisfied with his decision to dismantle the malthouse, although the success of any crop naturally depended on uncontrollable factors such as the weather. The winter of 1839-1840 had begun with a lot of rain and by 18 November 1839 Daniel informed his brother that he had sown only ten acres. By January 1840 he was anxious to start clearing the turnip fields but the weather kept changing and progress was slow. The following year the turnips were blighted with mildew and Daniel was afraid they would all rot. He began contemplating the farmer's lot: 'Such are the farmer's prospects, one day elated by the appearance of plenty, another day dejected by the appearance of scarcity. I thank God for all I possess'[92].

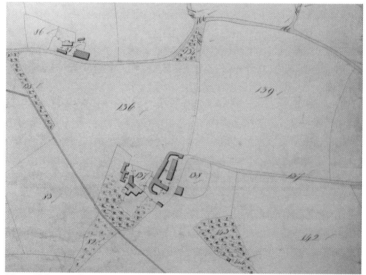

Detail from the 1841 tithe map showing the old Manor House and farm buildings shortly after Daniel Spurrell inherited the estate. Manor House Farm can be seen in the top left as well as two barns along the road, one of which has since been demolished.

From the 1840s onwards the day-to-day work on the estate and the names of the labourers are recorded in Daniel's labour account books, which have been preserved at the Norfolk Record Office. The farming year began in the autumn, when the land was ploughed and the winter crops were sown, and culminated in the harvest in August. Other late autumn or early winter jobs included clearing drains, carting turnips, pruning fruit trees and tending to the bullocks. The labourers worked six-day weeks and were paid fortnightly. There were a few occasions during the year when they were given a day off. On Christmas Day, after attending the morning service at church, Daniel usually hosted a meal for the men and boys. In 1872 he wrote that they 'dined at the Hall* on dumpling and beef and plum pudding and ale at 4 o'clock'[93]. Three years later, however, he decided that, since the men were paid double what they used to receive, there would be no Christmas dinner that year.

In the spring the workload picked up and it was not uncommon for women to join their husbands in the fields to earn additional income for the family (see end of chapter). In March 1866 several men were drilling, ploughing, harrowing or tending to the bullocks. Daniel sold his bullocks locally or sent them with a drover to London, where in March 1868 he sold two for £54. In the same month he began sowing a mix of ryegrass, trefoil, suckling and clover in the annual meadows.

The harvest was the main summer event on the farming calendar. A typical harvest day lasted from dawn to dusk and involved cutting, stacking and turning the corn and carting it back to the farmyard or the bullock

---

* Bessingham Manor House.

yard. On 5 September 1864 the men worked from 7 am till 10 pm, with one break for breakfast and another for dinner. The following day they went to the field called Wood Five Acres at 6.30 am to mow the barley, and then to Wood Eight Acres to turn over the wheat stacks before breakfast. After their break they managed to cart about eight loads of wheat from Wood Eight Acres before it began to rain. In 1869 Daniel used a threshing machine from Charles Le Neve of Sustead to thresh his wheat and barley. Earlier, in 1855, he had hired a Ransome's Steam Machine, which threshed and dressed about 380 coombs of wheat and about 180 coombs of barley.

The men's harvest wages were negotiated before the work began. In 1872 Thompson, Crow, Neal, Corbyn, Long, Leeder, W. Corbyn, Platten and Wright each had £7 5s. Mallett and Waterson were to have £5 10s 'but I was to judge their worth and behave liberally towards them'. Warner was to have £6, Emery £4 10s, Skivins 'to have what I think him worth, and Crow to have his wages doubled and something extra'[94]. Once all the hard work was over, the harvest could be celebrated with eating and drinking. Daniel noted that 26 September 1855 was a 'drinking day – harvest frolic last night'[95].

The 1876-1877 account book contains a list of the harvest dates and wages from 1852 to 1897. It shows that the harvest wages increased steadily from £5 10s to £8 in 1875, then fell in the following decade to £6 in 1885, and by 1895 had only risen to £6 10s. This was a consequence of the agricultural depression that hit Britain from the late 1870s onwards (see Chapter 11). Regular fortnightly wages also rose in the decades after 1840. An undated labour book from the 1840s shows that there were fourteen men on the books, with wages no higher than nine shillings per fortnight. By 1866 the average wage had doubled to between 17 and 20 shillings, with some men occasionally earning more according to seniority or the type of work they were doing. The total wage bill for 1869 was £425, about the same amount that Daniel contributed to the church restoration.

A strange incident occurred during the 1868 harvest when two men jumped out of a hot air balloon as it headed for an oak plantation in Bessingham. The balloon had taken off from Norwich market place and a strong wind in the south had propelled them towards Bessingham in fifteen minutes. As it approached the coast the men could hear 'confused noises from below, amongst which they could distinguish the barking of dogs, the lowing of cattle, the shouting of men, and the constant hum of thrashing machines,' to which was soon added 'the surge of the ocean'[96]. The balloonists tried to land but, since they were heading for the trees, they jumped out and let the balloon continue on its journey. It was last seen dropping into the sea off the coast of Sheringham.

Agriculture in Norfolk has typically focused on arable crops but animals were also kept in fairly large numbers, both as working animals (in the case of horses) and livestock. In 1855 Daniel listed the horses on the farm that year: Darling (born 1836), Jolly (1838), Bonny (1839), Dipper (1840), Smart (1841), Gypsey (1846), Proctor (1847), Beauty (1849), Boxer (1852), four colts and three foals. There were also five cows and about fifty bullocks in either the home yard or Bullard's yard in the north of the parish, which was accessed via a lane next to the pub. Daniel had 71 sheep and 28 lambs, as well as about 40 pigs. On 29 February 1888 Daniel listed his animals again. This time he had twelve cart horses in three teams, three riding horses, three ponies and eleven colts. There were seven cows (Cherry, Rosebud, Dolley, Snowball, Strawberry, Pevish and Sawny), 45 bullocks and five calves, 64 pigs, one bull and 99 sheep. The wool from the sheep was sold and in May 1875 a Mr. Neal was paid 32s 6d to wash and shear 'five score of sheep'[97]. Daniel also noted in the account book that he paid Neal an additional 1s 6d in beer money since shearers were entitled to three pints a day.

A gate by the ha-ha, used to move grazing animals and equipment in and out of the parkland.

Missing or stolen animals represented a potential loss of income for Daniel and in January 1842, when five sheep went astray, he offered £10 for their return or for information regarding the theft. The Aylsham Association and George Frankland each offered a further £5. There is no record of whether or not the sheep were found, but if they were stolen and the perpetrator was found, it is likely that the sentence would have been rather harsh by modern standards. The following year 21-year-old Robert Bacon stole a black gelding from the stables at the Manor House and was sentenced to nine months in gaol with hard labour. This seems lenient compared with the treatment that Timothy Puxley and Joseph Archer, aged 18 and 17 respectively, received in 1846. They had stolen some fowls from Timothy's father in Bessingham and whereas Timothy was sent to gaol for six months, Archer, who had a previous conviction, was transported (i.e. to Australia) for seven years. Newspaper reports of court proceedings show just how harsh the law was for what we might consider minor thefts in the village. In 1866 Ezra Duncan, a 25-year-old labourer, was sentenced to twelve months' hard labour after stealing a calico shirt from Robert Colman. Two years later Emily Burton, a 19-year-old field worker, broke into the house of Maria Frankland and stole a pair of boots, silk gloves, a handkerchief and waistband. Since she had previously stolen a leather purse from John Coleby, she was sentenced to six months' hard labour. Presumably many other crimes took place that were not reported, often to feed or clothe hungry children.

The farming year was interspersed with special events that enabled the community to come together and celebrate. In 1862 the Prince of Wales's wedding was marked with a party on the lawn in front of the old Manor House. It was attended by the labourers and their families and Daniel gave 2s 6d to each man and 1 shilling to each boy. Games such as camp, a version of football, were played and the winners received additional cash prizes. Half a barrel of stout was set up on the lawn and plum puddings were served. The next day, according to the account books, three men failed to turn up for work.

The villagers enjoyed many other forms of entertainment, from attending the local Aldborough fair to organising boxing, bowls and cricket matches. The pub had its own bowls team and in 1888 their season ended with prizes being handed out to the winners, including a teapot, cruet stand, toast rack and a pair of drinking horns.

~

In several households in the village, women would often seek casual work on farms, and although their wages were low, they could thereby earn extra income for their families. 'In Norfolk, as in most of the great arable areas, women's work was vital at weeding, hoeing, and stone picking, as well as at haymaking and harvest'[98]. In 1869 Elizabeth Neale was paid 12 shillings for picking mangels in the field called Eight Acres and at other times she docked corn or weeded. After Daniel Spurrell gave John and Charley Tuck a room at the Manor House, he paid Mrs. Bumphrey a shilling a week to do their laundry. In 1855 a girl in the Gotts family earned 3s 4d for five days of tilling, but domestic work was more usual for girls. Sarah Tipples and Mary Cole, both 15, were servants at the Manor House in 1841, for example.

Other women worked as dressmakers, laundresses, shopkeepers, teachers and even farmers. In 1861 Mary Amis was James Brooke's housekeeper in one of the cottages that later became The Den, but after his death in 1863 Mary took over his 14 acre farm and managed it with the help of a single labourer. On the 1891 census she

St. Mary's church, Bessingham. Restored in 1869, it retains
many original features, such as the 11ᵗʰ century round tower.

The farmhouse at Manor House Farm.

The former Horse Shoes Inn. For centuries villagers relaxed and socialised here or attended meetings. It closed its doors in 1959, having been part of the Bessingham estate since 1819.

Derelict farm buildings in the former parkland. A malthouse stood near here from the 1760s to the 1830s and the ruins of one, or possibly two, manor houses are also in this area.

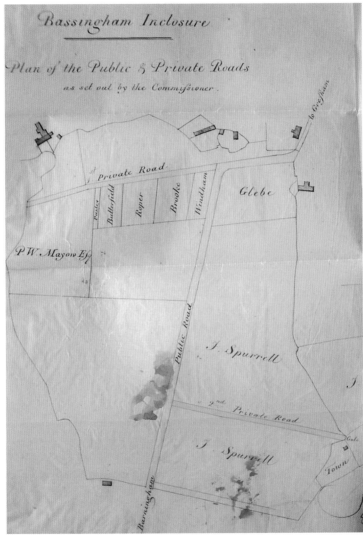

Map showing the allocation of the common land in 1822.
John Spurrell received the largest award, with smaller parcels
of land for P. W. Mayow, William Windham and the yeoman
farmers Snelling Roper, John Butterfield and James Brooke.

Charles Spurrell, painted c. 1820 by his uncle Robert Bourne Joy. Born in Bessingham, Charles spent most of his career as a brewer at Barclay Perkins & Co. in Southwark with his brother James, before retiring to Hill House, Dartford.

Catherine Case Copeman, painted by Emily Scott. Denham Spurrell was named after Dixon Denham, an African explorer related to Catherine's husband John Charles Denham.

A stained glass window in Roughton church in memory of
Sarah Joy, the last surviving member of the family that owned
and ran Roughton Mill from the 1770s until 1867. Daniel
Spurrell then inherited the mill before selling it in 1868 to
Benjamin Bond Cabbell.

A stained glass window in Bessingham church in memory of
Daniel and Sarah Frances Spurrell. The windows were
designed c. 1906 by the London firm of C. E. Kempe & Co.

Edmund Denham Spurrell with his dog Ruff, painted by the
Anglo-American artist James Jebusa Shannon in 1882.

Katherine Spurrell

Narcissus 'Katherine Spurrell', named after Katherine Anne
Spurrell by the daffodil breeder Edward Leeds. Katherine
bred at least 23 varieties of her own, some of which won the
R.H.S. Award of Merit. She planted several thousand bulbs at
The Den, which opened to the public after her death in 1919.

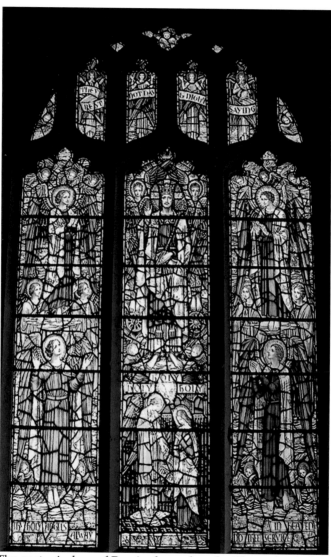

The east window of Bessingham church. The stained glass was designed by James Powell & Sons and installed in memory of Lt.-Col. Robert John Spurrell in 1932.

Albert Finch of Rose (now Finch) Cottage, painted in the 1960s by Mary l'Anson. Mary and her husband Bob Gamble purchased Bessingham Manor House and the parkland after the estate was broken up in 1970.

Yew Tree Cottage in 1977, for many years the home of the Mallett family.

Fiddlers Haven in 2016. Almost all of the cottages in the village have been refurbished in recent decades.

Detail from the 1988 aerial map of Norfolk. Most of the land is still under cultivation, but heavy machinery has now replaced the work of horses and people. To accommodate the tractors and combine harvesters, hedgerows have been removed and fields enlarged.

Bessingham Manor House and the ha-ha in 2008. The house and grounds had suffered years of neglect, particularly after the death of Mary Gamble in 1991.

The dining room of the Manor House in 2010. The wallpaper possibly dates from 1870. Note the window above the fireplace, which once looked out into the heated conservatory.

The tower at the entrance to the Manor House, designed in 1874 by Herbert Spurrell, with the walled garden behind.

Bessingham's new village sign, unveiled in 2012.

Bessingham Manor House in 2014, when it re-opened as self-catering holiday accommodation following a major programme of restoration.

Bessingham church by the local artist Martin Sexton. The village now attracts painters, walkers and church enthusiasts who all come to experience its landscape in their own way.

described herself as a 'retired farmer' and died three years later just after celebrating her 100th birthday. Her nephew William Cooper took over the lease and when he died in 1897 his widow Esther continued to farm the land until her death five years later.

Many women had to deal with husbands who were drunk or violent – or both. On 9 August 1862 George Frankland, once a successful butcher, came home drunk around 10 o'clock at night, swearing and accusing his wife Maria of having been with Henry White, the publican, and not giving him his dinner (i.e. lunch) that day. She explained that he did not turn up for his dinner but that his tea was now ready, whereupon he struck her on the back and pushed her towards the door, telling her to go back to Henry White. He calmed down and Maria began to serve his tea, but later he attacked her with a knife and tore her dress. About two weeks earlier he had been brought before the magistrates in Cromer after his wife accused him of using threatening language towards her. He had spent time in a lunatic asylum in the past but on this occasion he was examined by two doctors who found no signs of lunacy. The magistrates decided to bind him over to keep the peace for a month and Daniel Spurrell offered to be bound for him. However, following the incident that took place on the night of 9 August, which was witnessed by Sarah Anderson from outside the house, George Frankland was certified as a lunatic. The reasons stated for the decision were swearing (although George insisted he had been told fifteen years earlier in Norwich that 'damn' was not a swear word), writing sermons, not providing for his family, threatening to kill his wife, his rambling discourse and collecting things of no value. He was ordered to be removed immediately to the county asylum[99].

~

The censuses were taken every ten years from 1841 and listed everyone in the village along with their occupations. In 1841 there were five farmers (Daniel Spurrell, George Frankland, Timothy Puxley, George Emery and Robert Farrow) as well as a publican (Henry White), gardener (James Coleby), dressmaker (Sophia Broughton), shoemaker (John Grand with his apprentice Robert Emery), bricklayer (John Pearson), carpenter (Samuel Flogdell with his apprentice John Emery), laundress (Frances Skivens), thatcher (Timothy Puxley), fisherman (James Blyth), rough rider (John Beane), schoolmistress (Sarah Frankland), butcher (Thomas Frankland), and two housemaids and two farm boys (James Kirby, 15, and Furnival Bird, 11) at the Manor House. Ten years later three people were on parish relief (Samuel Partridge, John Blyth and Mary Pearson, all in their 70s and 80s) and there was also a turnip boy (George Green) and a colt breaker (Edward Youngman).

In 1861 the farmers included Daniel Spurrell, James Brooke at The Den, Timothy Puxley at Manor Farm and Samuel Thursby at Glebe Farm (now Rectory Cottage). George Green had been promoted from turnip boy to groom and by 1881 he was the coachman.

Chapter 8

MENS SANA IN CORPORE SANA

The Victorian period saw a great deal of progress in terms of education. All children were given the opportunity to go to school by the end of the nineteenth century and standards were rising universally. The earlier arrangement of informal dame schools and local grammar schools had evolved into a more rigorous system of village schools that catered for the children of labouring families, and more prestigious boarding schools for the sons of the gentry.

The church had always played an important role in education. William Johnson was Rector of Bessingham during the turbulent years from 1645 to 1657. The son of a Yorkshire shoemaker, he had studied at Gonville and Caius College, Cambridge, and was ordained in 1640 at the age of about 26. While at Bessingham he took in students, and James Tennant of Roughton, who later became a solicitor at Gray's Inn, is documented as being one of his pupils. A century later, in 1753, David Angus is recorded as being appointed schoolmaster at Bessingham.

In 1825 the Rev. Francis Arden, the curate, wrote to the Bishop of Norwich:

I am happy to say that our Bassingham School continues to flourish and that about thirty children are in daily attendance, most of those residing in the Parish, regularly attending at Church and being duly catechised and examined. I shall be much obliged to you to remit me the annual allowance of five pounds, retaining one for my annual subscription to the Clergy's Widows, which I will repay to the Schoolmistress[100].

The schoolmistress at the time was Sarah Frankland, who ran a dame school at Manor House Farm. Dame schools offered basic primary education for a small fee but they eventually disappeared after the provision of universal primary education came into force in the 1870s. Miss Frankland's establishment was a 'small school supported by subscriptions'[101] and in 1853 it still received a grant of £5 from the Diocese of Norwich to fund it. Two years earlier, according to the census, one pupil, Frances Curzon, aged six, was living with her at the school. The school was taken over by her sister Margaret, who had three pupils boarding with her in 1861 – Boson, Martha and Robert Denis. Martha was still with her in 1871, along with her sister Frances and a boy called Herbert Breese. Ten years later only one pupil – 6-year-old Charlotte Cooper from Bessingham – was boarding with her. When Margaret died in 1882 she was remembered as a 'faithful teacher of religion, industry and useful knowledge'[102].

After the passing of the Elementary Education Act in 1870, most children attended new schools that were run by local school boards. In February 1873 the Department of Education announced the formation of a school board for Gresham, Bessingham, North Barningham and East Beckham, and Daniel Spurrell was one of its earliest members. The school building, which was originally erected in 1856, was enlarged in 1873 at a cost of £560. In 1875 a byelaw stated that it was mandatory for children aged five to twelve to attend the school; those aged over ten could attend only 150 sessions if they were 'beneficially employed'[103].

In 1897 the board approved plans for the building of a new school and sent them to the Department of Education. Daniel's son Denham represented Bessingham on the board then along with Walter Frankland. Their names, together with those of James Page, the chairman, Samuel Pike and William Pyke, can still be seen on a plaque on the school wall, along with the names of the headmaster, architect and building contractor. The new school was intended to provide room for 50 infants and 128 juniors at a cost of £3,035, which the school board would repay to the Department of Education over 35 years.

In his report for 1897 the chairman of the board, James Page, spoke of education in the wider context of national interests: 'If England is to keep pace with Germany in her export trade to foreign countries and the colonies she must see to the education of the children and I do think the Government ought to supply the means so that the burden do (sic) not fall so hard on the ratepayers in the small school board districts'[104]. The average annual expenditure at Gresham village school was about £390 in 1897, or around 30 shillings per child, 20 shillings of which came from a government grant and the rest from the rates. The board had the power to take action against the parents of children who were absent from school, although very often this was on health grounds. Diphtheria, scarlet fever and measles all caused the school to close in the 1890s.

~

The local village school was rarely considered an option by the gentry. In the early 1800s the Spurrell family at Thurgarton, and probably at Bessingham too, had sent their sons to the Pottergate Street Academy in Norwich. As well as being educated in the classics, the boys were taught mathematics, natural philosophy, agriculture, commerce, bookkeeping and French, along with social refinements such as dancing, music and drawing. Surviving work 'suggests a first-rate middle-class private school'[105]. In 1818 William Dewing Spurrell, Daniel's cousin and heir to the Thurgarton estate, obtained a certificate for 'superior industry and application to his scholastic duties'[106] in the fourth class. William's younger brother Richard attended the school in the mid-1830s and was possibly Daniel's contemporary.

In his letters home Richard talked about studying Latin, physics, dancing and map drawing, and taking up flute lessons. He also played cricket and shot and went on school trips to Earlham and Lakenham. One Saturday in 1834 he and Daniel were accompanied by their uncle Daniel Towers Shears on a walk around the city, visiting the cathedral and St. Andrew's Hall.

By the middle of the century local grammar schools and private academies such as Pottergate were in decline. Many 'public' schools, which catered to pupils from all over the country, thanks in part to improvements in transportation, were founded or restructured around this time. They tended to provide a classical education, but also placed a strong emphasis on character-building and sports, because to Victorian educationalists a healthy body meant a healthy mind (*mens sana in corpore sana*).

Denham Spurrell was taught by the Rev. William Dalby at Sharrington Rectory before joining his elder brother Robert at Queen Elizabeth's School in Ipswich (now known as Ipswich School)*. The school had existed since Tudor times but in the 1840s had moved to a new purpose-built campus and its headmaster from 1858 to 1883, Dr. Hubert Ashton Holden, worked hard to build its reputation. The novelist Henry Rider Haggard, a contemporary of Robert and Denham at the school, remembered Holden as a 'charming and kindly gentleman,' but the school was a 'rough place, and there was much bullying of which the masters were not aware'[107]. Holden was aware of some bad behaviour, though, and although Denham was an excellent sportsman he was more likely to appear in Holden's punishment book than be praised for his academic achievements. His misdemeanours included losing his slippers, being late for or missing chapel, talking during morning prayer, and 'being concealed in a dormitory not his own'[108]. On many occasions his co-conspirator was

---

* I do not know why Daniel chose Ipswich but when I visited the school archives in 2010 I was surprised to discover a black-edged mourning card for his cousin Frances Shears, who died in 1878. Either one of his sons had left it at the school and it ended up in their archives, or it suggests a family connection with the school that I have so far been unable to discover.

none other than Holden's son. Their punishments included writing out psalms and lines from Virgil, or paying fines*.

In 1874 the *Ipswich Journal* noted that 'the attention now paid to athletic sports in public schools, if it has no other effect, does give the parents and guardians of the emulous youth very pleasant half-holidays to witness the young people disport themselves in light raiment, in all manner of forms of strong exercise'[109]. Daniel and Sarah attended sports day at the school several times and both gave away prizes for various competitions. In 1877 they were no doubt proud to see Denham win the mile race in 5 minutes and 3 seconds: 'Spurrell quickened his pace and came in first in fine style, indeed had not a visitor obstructed the path, we feel certain the time would have been under 5 minutes,' the school magazine reported[110].

Denham enthusiastically took part in a wide range of sports, including less well-known ones such as fives and quoits. He was elected captain of fives in 1877 and also served on the athletic committee. He enjoyed playing football and in April 1877 was described as 'a very fair side, though he should learn to kick at the proper time: a good runner'[111]. The previous year he had played in a football match against Ipswich Town, which the school lost. He also helped to organise paper chases around Ipswich at weekends and two maps have survived

---

* The punishment book was recently discovered in Bessingham and returned to Ipswich School after an absence of about 135 years. The school archivist, Dr. John Blatchly, concluded that Denham must have stolen the book and taken it home with him so that the headmaster would have no evidence of his mischief to present to his father.

showing the routes the boys took. They were divided into hounds and hares, the hares setting off on a pre-planned route, leaving pieces of paper along the way as scent for the hounds. The hares had to make it back to the school before the hounds caught them. The routes were long. On Saturday 9 March 1875 the hares had a ten minute start and finished in six hours, only five minutes ahead of the first hound. On Sunday 21 October 1876 the hares had a twenty minute start and took six and a half hours to complete the course, with two hounds fifteen minutes behind them[112]. This was not an official school sport but a form of entertainment devised by the boarders to occupy their time at the weekends.

Cricket was by far Denham's favourite sport. In November 1876 the school magazine reported that he 'has improved in batting, rather stiff, and wants confidence. A fair wicket-keeper'[113]. In August of the following year the school beat Coltishall 'due to steady play from E. D. Spurrell'[114], who scored 14 of the school's 53 runs. That month the cricketers rose early one day and journeyed to North Norfolk, 'but a long drive through the Norfolk scenery on a summer's morning can scarcely be called a hardship'[115]. They played the Gunton Club at Suffield Park that day and Holt the following day. When school resumed after the summer holidays Denham had been elected captain of the cricket team.

Robert was a good sportsman too, having captained the cricket team three years before his brother. After leaving Ipswich he went up to Trinity Hall, Cambridge, and in 1876 rowed in the Oxford and Cambridge University Boat Race. The school magazine reported that the race 'has an especial interest for us Ipswichians this year'[116]. Cambridge lost but when he returned to the school in October 1876 for a Past versus Present cricket match, with his brother on the opposing team, Robert was no doubt congratulated on his effort.

After leaving school Denham returned to Bessingham and on several occasions took part in cricket matches in the grounds of the Manor House. On 30 July 1881 Bessingham played Gresham. Denham was third out to bat and scored 42 runs but the result was a tie: 102 runs apiece. He took a keen interest in school cricket throughout his life. His obituary in *The Ipswichian* said he would 'chiefly be remembered by living O.I.s for the unfailing regularity with which he turned up, year by year, to watch the O.I. Cricket Match'[117].

Denham Spurrell (seated, third from left) at a cricket match at Ipswich School in 1948, in which former captains played the school's current First XI. Denham did not play but as the oldest living former captain he spun the coin.

He was an active alumnus, serving as president of the Old Ipswichians in 1932. In 1951, at the age of 93, he was sent some old photographs by the school in the hope that he would be able to recognise the faces, but his housekeeper, Martha Douglas Powell, replied saying that his sight was failing and he could not recognise anyone. Otherwise, she added, 'Mr. Spurrell is really very well for his years'[118].

PART FOUR

1890 ~ 1952

Chapter 9

A LONG-LIVED RACE

Denham Spurrell's life began in the 1850s and lasted until the 1950s and during that time he witnessed a huge amount of change. The ascendancy of the Victorian gentry in local affairs was beginning to be challenged at the end of the nineteenth century. The agricultural depression had reduced their incomes, the introduction of death duties had struck a blow to their financial security, and the democratisation of local government had led to a noticeable shift in power at the parish and district levels. Only half of the families featured in the 1863 edition of *Burke's Landed Gentry* were still in the 1914 edition.

Denham was born at the old Manor House on 7 October 1858. He was christened Edmund Denham but was always known by his middle name. The name Edmund appears several times on both the Flaxman and Joy family trees but I do not know if he was named after anybody in particular. His middle name was after Dixon Denham, the African explorer who served briefly as Governor of Sierra Leone in the 1820s. Denham Spurrell's maternal aunt, Catherine Case Copeman, had married John Charles Denham, a Treasury clerk who was also a watercolour artist*. John Charles Denham was Dixon Denham's cousin and perhaps the latter's African adventures had appealed to Daniel, who had produced that remarkably good map of Africa in the 1830s.

After leaving school (see Chapter 8) Denham Spurrell dived into the North Norfolk sporting scene. He later listed his recreations as 'sport, hunting and shooting, etc.'[119] and this seems to have been the case throughout his life. In 1878, just after his 20th birthday, he became secretary of the Gunton Hunt and in the following decade was Master of the North Norfolk Harriers. For several years the club's forty hounds were kept in kennels at Bessingham and one of the whips was Robert Emery, who was also a groom at the Manor House. In 1885 the Harriers met on Mondays and Thursdays and often set out from the Manor House and other local places. In March 1889, for example, about twenty-two ponies met at Thurgarton Hall† and 'had a very good run and kill'[120]. Denham was also a 'first-class shot'[121] and regularly organised shoots on the estate. On 9 January 1889 he was one of a party of five that bagged six pheasants, seven moorhens, two partridges, a rabbit and seven pigeons. Later that month Robert Purdy (who, according to his grandson, spent most of the time from October until the end of January each year with a gun under his arm) joined him in Roughton, returning home with four

---

* A few years ago I discovered that an album containing some of his paintings and drawings had ended up at Yale University in the United States, and while visiting my wife's family not far from there I took the opportunity to view the album.
† It is unclear whether this means Thurgarton Hall or Thurgarton House.

pheasants and two rabbits. John Tuck would sometimes accompany Denham when he went for a walk, taking a gun with him; on 25 January 1889 Denham recorded his disappointment at having bagged only a partridge, a hare, a rabbit and three pigeons on one of these walks. The largest number of animals bagged by a shooting party hosted by Denham is 109 on 5 November 1919: eighty-nine pheasants, one partridge, four hares, five rabbits, eight woodcocks, one pigeon and one moorhen. In 1914 Denham shot a 'female pheasant in male plumage'[122] at Bessingham, which he donated to the Norwich Castle Museum.

Denham Spurrell, with hounds probably belonging to the North Norfolk Harriers.

Denham enjoyed other sports too. On several occasions he travelled by train to watch football matches.

In March 1889 he watched Norfolk beat Cambridge and Wymondham beat Lynn. Later in life he enjoyed the more relaxing game of bowls and in his final years would invite friends over for a game every Wednesday.

He had an extremely busy social life as a bachelor, attending balls and dinner parties and often taking John Tuck with him if he spent the night in Norwich. When in London in January 1889 he called on his old school friend Henry Rider Haggard but he was out, although he did see Haggard's wife and children*. Whilst in the capital he attended Macknamara's Ball at Westminster Town Hall but 'did not feel inclined for dancing and went home early'[123]. Later in the same month he went to a dinner party hosted by Sir Alfred Jodrell at Bayfield Hall, returning home at 6 o'clock in the morning, as well as the Cinderella Ball and the Bachelor's Ball in Norwich, taking Marion Philpott and the two Misses Ives with him to the latter.

In spite of the plentiful female company and the fact that a Miss Bainbridge had caught his eye earlier in the month ('thought her very pretty and jolly'[124]), Denham was in love with Margy Wilson, the daughter of the Rev. James Wilson, who had been Vicar of St. Stephen's, Norwich, since leaving Barningham in 1875. The two families were close. Margy's father had officiated at the wedding of Denham's eldest sister in 1879, and one of her brothers officiated at another sister's funeral in 1931.

---

* The friendship between the two families continued in the next generation. Rider Haggard's daughter Lilias dedicated her delightful book *Norfolk Life* to 'Margaret [Spurrell], who knows so many of the joys and sorrows of the years here chronicled'[125]. Margaret was the daughter of one of Denham's cousins.

Denham called on Margy at the Vicarage on 7 January 1889, waiting for her to come home, but had no luck. A few days later he wrote to her asking to meet at Chapelfield at the rather precise time of 4.35 that afternoon, but she did not show up. A few days later Margy was in North Norfolk but Denham missed her again: 'Kitty told me Margy was at the Aldborough concert last Wednesday and that she was staying at Barningham. Sent a note to her by Emery which he brought back as Margy had left for home again last Saturday'[126]. Finally on the 17th he had better luck, recording in his diary that they met in Norwich and that Margy 'went for a little turn with me, etc., etc.'[127]. Whatever the 'etc.' meant, the relationship did not go any further and by April Denham seems to have taken a shine to Margy's sister Mary, who had come to stay at Bessingham for a few days. One afternoon, after a walk around the village, they drove to Roughton to pick flowers in the woods.

Denham's life was not only a never-ending round of social calls and bachelors' balls. His father began to instruct him in the running of the estate and in 1889 gave him the job of paying the men. That year Denham visited Billockby to oversee some work being done there. He also called on labourers who were unwell. In February 1889 he visited George Crow, who had been off work for some time. Crow still looked very ill so later in the day Denham sent him a bottle of port to cheer him up.

During the 1890s he began to devote more time to civic duties and served on the newly formed parish and district councils (see Chapter 10) and the local school board. He was a churchwarden too and a lay representative at meetings of the Diocese of Norwich. He also joined the Norfolk Imperial Yeomanry, a volunteer cavalry force founded in 1901. Most of the officer ranks were filled by members of the local gentry and Denham served as a lieutenant. He attended various parades and training sessions and was presented to the King after the Yeomanry escorted the royal party to Sandringham in November 1901. But the strict regime did not suit Denham. He had signed up for three years and was expected to attend twelve drills a year and an annual training session, but he often failed to turn up. Many years later he admitted to Ted Finch, who grew up in Bessingham before the Second World War, that he had been 'drummed out'[128], although the official record states less embarrassingly that he resigned his commission in 1904 once his three-year term was up.

Officers of the Norfolk Imperial Yeomanry at Cromer in 1903. Lt. Denham Spurrell is standing, top right.

One event in Bessingham's history that is still talked about today is the bear that Denham's brother Robert brought back from India in the 1890s.

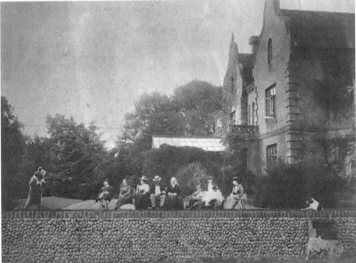

The famous bear of Bessingham, sketched (above) in 1893 by the Rev. R. J. Simpson, Rector of Metton and Felbrigg, and photographed (below); seated are Denham Spurrell (far left), Daniel and Sarah Spurrell (centre) and other family members.

The bear was captured on camera and drawn by a local clergyman, who described it as 'tame'[129]. It wasn't entirely tame, though, because it had to be put down, probably after escaping and attacking someone in the village. The exact details are unclear and several versions exist. According to one account, Denham was attacked by the bear when it was in its cage. According to another, the bear escaped and attacked a housemaid. And according to yet another story, it made its way into the cottage of a lady who, being blind, thought it was a guest and made it a cup of tea.

~

Daniel celebrated his 80th birthday in 1897 and by now he had already passed on the management of the estate to his son*. He lived for almost another decade. He and his wife Sarah were both born in 1817 and both passed away in Holy Week, 1906, aged 89 and 88 respectively, spending their final years at the Manor House with several unmarried children for company. Sarah was also looked after by a companion, Alice Mills, her daughter's step-daughter. Daniel was in good health until his final days. 'He had been ill and confined to bed, but on Wednesday morning, feeling better, announced his intention of getting up. This, however, he never did, for in less than an hour he passed peacefully away,' his obituary noted[130]. His son-in-law, the Rev. William Woodward Mills, and the Rector of Bessingham, the Rev.

---

* On the 1901 census Daniel described himself as a 'retired agriculturalist,' implying that agriculture to him was an art or a science and not just a business.

E. H. Taylor, officiated at the funeral, which took place on Easter Saturday. Friends, family, neighbours, tenants and labourers were all present. Sarah outlived her husband by three days and died four hours before his funeral. At her own funeral the altar was decorated by Alice Mills and the Rector spoke fondly of the elderly couple: 'In many ways their lives were an example for good, from which all might learn something'[131]. The *Eastern Daily Press* said that Daniel came from a 'long-lived race' and continued:

> None who viewed the two coffins side by side, the one placed there on Saturday and the other just then lowered, and reflected how after long honoured years, even in "death were not divided," the aged and worthy couple who began life in the selfsame year, could think other than that they were indeed happy in the manner of their passing hence after a union of five and fifty years[132].

~

Daniel left the Bessingham estate to Denham along with Flaxman's Farm in Roughton. His will was witnessed by his cousin Richard Spurrell of Thurgarton House and by John Tuck, a reminder of the bond of loyalty and trust that existed between the two men.

Seven months after inheriting the estate, Denham married Emily Marten (née Finch) at St. Stephen's Church in Westminster at the age of 48. There are two principal reasons why this might have happened after his parents had passed away. One is that they disagreed with the marriage. Emily was ten years older than Denham, which may not have met with their approval. But I believe the reason has something to do with the fact that Denham was the first owner of the Bessingham estate to be hit by the new estate duty, which had been introduced in 1894. Emily had been left several thousand pounds when her first husband died in 1904 and had probably known Denham for a while (her sister had married into the Copeman family). Many estates had to be broken up or sold as a result of the so-called death duties, but Emily was willing to help Denham to avoid this happening to the Bessingham estate. Another reason for concluding this is that she did not live with Denham at Bessingham*. She had her own residence at Oval Cottage in Rye, Sussex, and also spent time at the Ladies' Army and Navy Club near Piccadilly in London. When she died in 1922 she left £25,000. Most of this went to the children of her brothers and sisters but Denham received a specific bequest of £1,000 as well as some furniture, china, pictures and books. The residue, which probably amounted to a few thousand pounds, was to be held in trust for Denham's use during his lifetime.

As his father's heir Denham also became lord of the manor of Bessingham, which by now was a largely meaningless title. He made a few additions to the estate, including 35 acres of glebe land, which he bought from the church for £1,000 in 1907, and three further parcels of land purchased from Col. Barclay of Hanworth Hall in

---

* Several people I interviewed, who remember Denham Spurrell as an old man during their childhood, thought he was a bachelor his whole life.

1909. He continued to enjoy the usual interests of a country gentleman: hunting, shooting and entertaining, as well as eating, drinking and socialising at his clubs. He was a member of the Cromer Club House (now the Victoria Court Hotel), which was built in 1899 and patronised by the Prince of Wales, and he chaired a meeting in 1923 to wind up the club voluntarily. He was also a member of the Norfolk and Norwich Club and the Primrose Club in London, which was affiliated with the Conservative Party.

He was the first person in Bessingham to own a car, which he purchased from Mann Egerton in Norwich in 1907. The car came with a chauffeur, Sidney Abigail. John Tuck's daughter Myrtle explained many years later that 'the chauffeur came to stay with us and that is how I met my husband'[133]. Denham later learned to drive, although his motoring abilities often left his passengers a little shaken. Roy Street, who visited his cousins at Glebe Cottage when he was a boy, remembers having his eyes shut most of the time when Denham offered to drive him somewhere. Rather embarrassingly for somebody who was once their chairman, Denham was brought before the magistrates at Cromer in 1946 and found guilty of 'driving without due care'[134]. He had crossed the Holt-Cromer road on his way to Sheringham without looking, causing another vehicle to swerve and crash. He apparently said that the other car should have stopped because everyone knew that he always drove to Sheringham at the same time every week. The *Evening Standard* reported that 87-year-old Denham was then one of Britain's oldest motorists*. He was fined £3 and

---

* He was actually 88 when the article was written.

disqualified from driving until he passed a test. He told the newspaper that he had sent in his application and considered himself a better motorist than ever because he drove slowly and carefully. He did not want to waste his men's time driving him around and since he had a lot of business to see to he wanted to be able to drive again. He said he was fit and active and that driving helped him stay young. He claimed he did not need glasses and was not bothered by driving at night.

Denham Spurrell with his car outside the Manor House.

It is as a small man with a white moustache, wearing a tweed jacket and flat cap and carrying a cane, that Denham is fondly remembered by people alive today who knew him when they were children in the 1930s and 1940s. They affectionately called him Old Denham, but never to his face. He was often seen walking or riding along the lanes, checking to see that everything was in order on the estate. Most people in the village respected him. They found him to be a pleasant man who looked after the village and his tenants. But Denham also believed that people had their place. The headmaster of the village school at Gresham wrote to him suggesting that he might want to subsidise Ted Finch's fees at Paston Grammar School in North Walsham. Ted and his parents were not aware of this, and Ted was taken aback when Denham spotted him in the village one day and told him he had ideas above his station. But Denham could be sympathetic too. Ted's parents, Albert and Rosa Finch, began renting Rose Cottage (now called Finch Cottage) on Valentine's Day 1920. The monthly rent was 8s 4d, which was raised to 10s 4d the following year. In 1927 they got behind with their payments but Denham was understanding and it was not until 1929 that they caught up again[135].

In the 1940s Denham began taking flying lessons and made a few short trips over the estate and out over the North Sea. A memorable event in the post-war years was his flight (as a passenger) to Bournemouth and back in October 1949. Several people alive today remember gathering in a field on the estate to watch the plane return at 5 o'clock one afternoon and welcome Denham home. The previous day, after Denham's first attempt had been cancelled by the pilot on account of the 'wild grey sky,' Denham sat by the 'cosy warmth of a log fire,' watching the trees in the parkland sway in the wind, and told a journalist why he wanted to make the journey. 'I can't go long distances by car and it is much too roundabout to go by rail. I can't go long journeys at my age, but by air I can get there and back in a day'[136]. Dan Burgess flew Denham and his travel companion Mrs. Dent to Bournemouth in four hours – a longer than expected journey due to a petrol stop and strong headwinds. There Denham visited the widow of an old school friend but was anxious to return home so that he would not disappoint the waiting crowd – and also so as not to lose a bet. His neighbour at Barningham Hall, Sir Charles Mott-Radclyffe, had bet ten shillings that he would not make it back the same day. The plane touched down near Thurgarton church at 5 o'clock and Denham posed for a photograph with the pilot and George Whortley, who had arranged the trip for him. He claimed that he had enjoyed every minute of the flight and 'felt no ill effects,' adding 'I could now go and do another journey like it'[137].

Denham Spurrell with Jim Crampton and Dan Burgess in front of the plane in which he flew to Bournemouth and back in 1949 to visit the widow of an old school friend.

John Tuck, now a nonagenarian like Denham, was disappointed that he could not make it to see his old employer touch down. For ninety years the two men had seen each other on almost a daily basis and even lived in the same house as boys, but the class structure was such that their relationship would have remained professional. It is interesting to think how the changes of the previous century had affected their lives in different ways. John Tuck spent his final years knowing that his grandchildren and great-grandchildren would have much greater opportunities than he did. He had a state pension and free access to healthcare, which his parents, even if they had not died young, would not have lived to enjoy. These things would have been less important for Denham, for whom the joys of living the life of a country gentleman were now curbed by rationing and the unwillingness of young girls to go into service.

But his final years were not at all melancholy. He had relished adventure in various forms all his life and as he aged and became less agile he made sure that he surrounded himself with younger and more energetic companions. Fred and Olive Hudson's daughter Nell spent a lot of time playing at the Manor House as a girl. She would push Denham around the garden in his wheelchair, play the piano while he sang, have tea parties in the tower by the entrance to the driveway, or listen to 'Dick Barton Special Agent' on the radio in Denham's study. She helped with odd tasks too, such as scrubbing the hall floor or picking flowers from the garden when Denham was having guests. One year Denham took her to the Norfolk Show and she recalls the freedom of being able to wander around with a member's ticket. Watching the show jumping from the grandstand was a special treat. When Nell was awarded a scholarship to Paston Grammar School in North Walsham, Denham gave her mother some money for a jacket and skirt from Bond's of Norwich as a reward for her achievement.

When Denham was without a housekeeper, Ruby Wiseman, whose husband was the farm manager, lent a hand, preparing his midday meals. Her daughter Rosie would help during the school holidays and took Denham his coffee after lunch. When she went back to collect the tray she would invariably find a Quality Street chocolate under the saucer, 'a real treat in the time of rationing'[138]. The smell of good coffee still brings this memory back to her.

Denham also enjoyed the company of Jock Lane, an agricultural student who came to Norfolk in the summer of 1950 to learn about farming. He worked for the Batts (whose son Christopher he knew from school) at Gresham Hall as well as Sir Charles Mott-Radclyffe at Barningham Hall and John Neill at Thurgarton Hall. He lodged first with the Batts' estate manager Geoffrey Stibbons and his wife Gwen, and later with Gwen's sister Olive Hudson at Glebe Cottage. Olive arranged for Jock to go up to the Manor House once a week for a bath and afterwards he would stay and chat with Denham. He grew fond of him and remembers Denham giving him £21 on his twenty-first birthday.

At the end of his life Denham became increasingly frail and spent more and more time in his study. A bed was brought in and, surrounded by prints of typical country scenes that reminded him of all the years spent in the saddle or at the peg, he lived out his final days by the warmth of the large fireplace, reading and smoking his pipe. Maurice Wiseman prepared meals for him to eat in his room. Just after Christmas 1951 he began suffering painful cramps in his arms and legs and on the morning of Saturday, 5 January 1952 he passed away. He was cremated at Horsham St. Faith and a memorial service was later held at Bessingham, attended by relatives, farm workers and other villagers.

~

Denham was the last surviving member of the Bessingham branch of the Spurrell family. His eldest sister, Emily, had married the Vicar of Aylmerton, the Rev. William Woodward Mills, in 1879. Mills had been born in Trinidad in the West Indies and arrived in Norfolk in the 1870s. After his first wife died he married Emily, who was a doting step-mother to his young children and gave birth to three more of her own: Dorothy Sarah Spurrell (Sally), Ursula Blanche and Geoffrey Daniel Spurrell (Daniel). Emily dutifully performed the public and private roles of a clergyman's wife and also stood for election to the district council in the 1890s (see Chapter 10). She died in 1905, a year after receiving the devastating news that her 18-year-old son had been killed in an accident in South Africa. Daniel Mills had followed his half-brother Henry to the mining town of Barberton and was killed in a trolley accident near the entrance to the Sheba mine. The trolley derailed and Daniel hit his head, dying immediately. Another passenger, James Holden, later succumbed to his injuries and a gravestone was erected in memory of them both in Barberton. Daniel's parents also placed a memorial inside Aylmerton church.

A memorial to Daniel Spurrell's grandson Daniel Mills, who died in an accident in South Africa in 1904.

Neither Sally nor Ursula married but lived together for many years at the Old Mill House in Roughton, their great-grandmother's childhood home. They ran a poultry farm and were deeply involved in the local community. Ursula died in 1949 having dedicated much of her time to the local nursing association and Women's Institute and serving on the parish and district councils and local school board. After her death her friends 'thought of her garden which she had tended and loved; of the beautiful needlework that she excelled in; we thought of all her interests and thoughts for others. And so we left her, rejoicing for her that now her spirit was freed to a greater and even more glorious life'[139]. Her sister Sally remained at the Old Mill House until her death fifteen years later*.

Denham's second sister, Blanche, spent most of her adult life at Old Cottage in Heacham, but was buried at Bessingham in 1931. The Rev. Thomas Erskine Wilson, the brother of Denham's old flame Margy, officiated. In her will Blanche mentioned a Reynolds painting and a grand piano she had already given to her brother Robert.

Katherine (Kitty), Denham's third sister, lived in Bessingham her whole life and was a respected daffodil grower. A variety was named after her by the celebrated daffodil breeder Edward Leeds, who died in 1877 when Kitty was in her 20s. At the Daffodil Conference in 1890 the *Manchester Courier* described Narcissus 'Katherine Spurrell' as one of the best exhibits and it became a popular choice for gardeners in the late nineteenth century. The Spurrell family in general had a keen interest in gardening at this time. The 1870 summer show of the local horticultural society, held at Baconsthorpe Rectory, contained 'a charming basket of wildflowers arranged by some of the younger members of the family of D. Spurrell, Esq., of Bessingham, of which older adepts would have no reason to be ashamed'[140]. Two years later,

---

* She left the house to Philip and Diana Hayward, who were family friends. When I met Diana in 2010 to talk about Roughton Mill and her memories of the Mills sisters I was surprised and honoured to be given a box of paintings and photographs that Diana had found at the Old Mill House and hung onto for almost 50 years, not knowing what to do with them. They included a portrait of Catherine Case Copeman by Emily Scott and another of Charles Spurrell (my great-great-great-grandfather) by his uncle Robert Bourne Joy.

in one of the letters sent to her cousin Charles, Kitty's sister Mary said she had been 'doing a great deal of gardening and that sort of thing'[141].

Of all the sisters it was Kitty who had the greenest fingers. By the 1880s she was writing to the widely read periodical *The Garden* with reports of the plants growing at Bessingham Manor House. One spring she described the flowers in bloom, stating that 'there are so many things budding up in the well-stored garden' at Bessingham, particularly double-yellow wallflowers[142]. In another letter she gave a very detailed 'outline of our chrysanthemum culture at Bessingham'[143]. In 1901 she won her first Award of Merit from the Royal Horticultural Society for a daffodil variety named 'Major Spurrell' after her brother Robert. 'Agnes Harvey' (1902) and 'Caroline Carver' (1903) also received the Award of Merit and 'F. C. J. Spurrell' won the Bronze Flora Medal at an R. H. S. garden show in 1906. Three years later she presented a bulb called 'Mrs. Daniel Spurrell' to the Narcissus Committee but it did not meet their approval. In all she grew at least twenty-three cultivars, mostly named after family and friends. Apart from 'Agnes Harvey' most of Kitty's daffodils were not grown or sold in large numbers. Some fetched high prices: in a 1908 bulb catalogue 'Major Spurrell' was the most expensive item at 84 shillings per bulb. It is possible that some of her rare daffodils still bloom in Bessingham every spring.

When Kitty's father died in 1906 he stated in his will that she would receive all the 'garden plants and implements'[144]. A planting book from the following year lists forty rows of bulbs grown by Kitty in the walled garden, some of which were sold to a nursery. The rows included 'Katherine Spurrell' and an 'Old Bessingham' double jonquil.

In 1912, at the age of sixty, Kitty married her cousin Flaxman Charles John Spurrell, a shy hard-working archaeologist – the same 'F. C. J. Spurrell' who had had a daffodil named after him a few years earlier, and the same archaeologist who had catalogued the Roman coins discovered at Baconsthorpe in 1878. He also excavated and wrote about sites in Kent, where he spent most of his life, and recorded and described hundreds of artefacts that his friend William Flinders Petrie sent home from Egypt.

Flaxman Charles John Spurrell (second from left) exploring a denehole in Kent in the 1860s with his father Flaxman (far left) and other amateur archaeologists.

In 1896, after his mother's death, Flaxman became increasingly reclusive and pessimistic and retired to

Norfolk, occupying a bedroom and sitting room at the Manor House before The Den was converted into a private house for his own use. According to Petrie:

> The entreaties of his friends would not lead him out, and for the last twenty years he seldom came from his retirement in Norfolk. Once and again he would suddenly appear for an hour or two, in a way tantalizing to those who remembered the keen interests of the past which he could no longer be induced to continue[145].

He spent his days reading in the tower that overlooked the walled garden where Kitty was often to be found, and it is wonderful to imagine them falling in love among the daffodils in their old age. They were married at Bessingham church in 1912. Flaxman drove there in his landau while Kitty walked in her gardening clothes and straw hat. They lived at The Den for a few short years until Flaxman died in 1915, and Kitty remained there until her death in 1919. Much of Flaxman's personal collection of archaeological artefacts was donated to the Natural History Museum in London and the Norwich Castle Museum. At The Den Kitty naturalised thousands of bulbs. After her death the grounds were opened to the public for a short time. An announcement in the *Gardener's Chronicle* mentioned a staggering 10,000 daffodils in bloom, 'all grown by the celebrated raiser of Narcissi, the late MRS. CATHERINE (sic) SPURRELL'[146]. These included 'Major Spurrell,' 'Agnes Harvey' and many other varieties that were popular at the time.

Denham's youngest sister, Mary Isabelle, married a London solicitor but returned to North Norfolk after his death in 1930. She lived with her brother at Bessingham Manor House in the 1930s but passed away in Sheringham in 1948, a few days after her 91st birthday (see Chapter 13 for further details).

~

Denham's elder brother Robert entered the army in 1878 after leaving Cambridge. Two years later he resigned his commission as a lieutenant in the East Norfolk Regiment and joined the 3rd Dragoon Guards as a cavalry officer. He was posted to India and spent two decades there. In 1891 he was elected a member of the Cavalry and Guards Club in London, having been proposed by his fellow officer Major William Utting Cole*. The life of a cavalry officer in India was one of considerable leisure and Robert enjoyed playing polo and hunting big game. He wrote a short story for his nephew Daniel Mills entitled *Shikar, A Humorous Tiger*. While stationed in India he married Mary Maude, the daughter of Major-General James Lawtie Fagan.

He did not spend all his time on the polo field or in the jungle, however. He took part in the Hazara expedition of 1891 and the North West Frontier and Tirah campaigns of 1897-1898. In 1892 he had been transferred to the 5th Royal Irish Lancers and was promoted to the rank of captain, becoming a major in 1896. During the Tirah

---

* Cole was related to the Copeman family and his daughter Anne married Neville Chamberlain (Prime Minister, 1937-1940).

campaign he served as Chief Transport Officer on the Lines of Communication and temporary Acting Quartermaster General. Photographs from Robert's time in India show him posing with other officers or standing on the parade ground with his men.

Maj. Robert John Spurrell (middle row, second from right) with fellow officers of the 5th Royal Irish Lancers in India in 1897.

When the Second Boer War broke out in 1899 the 5th Lancers were sent to South Africa. Robert commanded a squadron that saw action in 1901 in Barberton (where his nephew later died). The Lancers were also caught up in the famous siege of Ladysmith and Robert's wife coordinated efforts to send them clothes, pipes and tobacco.

After the Boer War Robert returned to England. He was garrisoned briefly in Norwich in 1903 with the 3rd Provisional Dragoon Guards before being sent to

Aldershot. He was placed on retirement pay in 1905, a year before his father's death. Marion Philpott wrote in 1927 that 'most unhappy family disagreements estranged the two brothers – though both are still living they never meet'[147]. Denham had taken over the management of the Bessingham estate while Robert was in India, but Robert was the elder son and perhaps he expected that the estate would be left to him anyway. As it turned out, he was given the Billockby Hall estate while Denham inherited Bessingham and perhaps this was the cause of their disagreement.

Maj. Robert John Spurrell (seated, third from right) with fellow officers of the 3rd Provisional Dragoon Guards in Norwich in 1903.

With the help of a £3,000 loan from his sister Blanche, Robert purchased Glandyfi Castle and 42 acres of land near Aberystwyth on the Welsh coast. He and Mary planted rhododendrons, azaleas, mountain laurels, acers and magnolias in the grounds. The property also contained a tennis court and croquet lawn and a landing stage on the River Dovey. Robert lived the life of a country gentleman at Glandyfi Castle but after the outbreak of the First World War he felt it was his duty to return to the army. He was promoted to the rank of lieutenant-colonel and given command of the 13th battalion of the Royal Sussex Regiment, which arrived on the Western Front in November 1915. The scale and horror of the fighting was like nothing he had experienced as a cavalry officer in India. At the age of 60 he was considered too old to command a modern infantry battalion effectively and in March 1916 he was appointed Commandant on the Lines of Communication, based at the infantry depot in Etaples. In his war memoirs Neville Bulwer-Lytton, later the 3rd Earl of Lytton, wrote of an encounter with Robert while convalescing at a military hospital in Le Touquet after suffering injuries during a shelling raid. He described Robert's disappointment at being forced to relinquish command of his battalion.

> This was a bitter blow to [Robert], for he
> was a frightfully keen soldier, brave as a
> lion and gorgeously handsome. I don't
> think I ever saw a man so like my idea of
> Thackeray's Colonel Newcome. The
> sympathy which he showed me on this
> occasion was perfectly delightful; he

insisted upon taking me as soon as I was able to walk to Holy Communion. It is many years since I have practised any form of religion, and it seems to me irreverent to partake of holy mysteries if you don't believe in them; but he, so to speak, ordered me to go and I saw that it would hurt him seriously if I refused. Throughout the service I watched his splendid face touched with the deepest emotion, and it was one of the most beautiful sights I have ever seen; besides, I felt so proud that he should show the affection of a father to me. Later he visited us in the line, and his visit happened to coincide with a small German attack on my company front. When the whole thing was over I found him standing by my side on the fire step. The trenches were then in a frightful state of slough, and I think he realised it would have been impossible for him at the age of sixty to be an infantry Colonel[148].

He left Etaples in June 1917 and returned to England. His obituary in *The Times* refers to 'an illness contracted on active service during the Great War, and borne courageously for 12 years,'[149] and his memorial in Bessingham church mentions '12 years of intense illness borne with unfailing courage from illness contracted in the Great War'[150]. These are almost certainly references to shell shock, or post-traumatic stress disorder as it would be diagnosed today.

Robert may have sought solace in his garden and pastimes, and was supported by his devoted wife. Whether for financial or other reasons, Glandyfi Castle was put on the market in 1927, boasting electric lights and central heating, but it did not sell. Robert died in August 1929 and his widow Mary made another attempt to sell the property in October of that year, perhaps as a way of raising money to cover the death duties. Once again it remained unsold and the following year Mary decided instead to put several paintings from her and Robert's families up for auction.

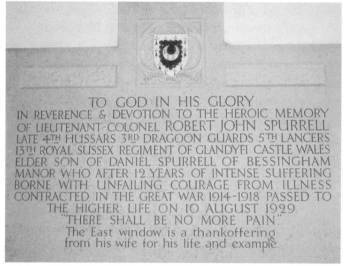

TO GOD IN HIS GLORY
IN REVERENCE & DEVOTION TO THE HEROIC MEMORY
OF LIEUTENANT-COLONEL ROBERT JOHN SPURRELL
LATE 4TH HUSSARS 3RD DRAGOON GUARDS 5TH LANCERS
13TH ROYAL SUSSEX REGIMENT OF GLANDYFI CASTLE WALES
ELDER SON OF DANIEL SPURRELL OF BESSINGHAM
MANOR WHO AFTER 12 YEARS OF INTENSE SUFFERING
BORNE WITH UNFAILING COURAGE FROM ILLNESS
CONTRACTED IN THE GREAT WAR 1914-1918 PASSED TO
THE HIGHER LIFE ON 10 AUGUST 1929.
"THERE SHALL BE NO MORE PAIN."
The East window is a thankoffering
from his wife for his life and example.

Memorial to Lt.-Col. Robert John Spurrell in Bessingham
church; the arms are of Trinity Hall, Cambridge.

The Castle remained in her possession until her death in 1942*. In most of the intervening years Mary had

---

* It is now a Bed & Breakfast.

130

placed 'In Memoriam' announcements in *The Times* on the anniversary of her husband's death. Robert was buried in Bessingham churchyard and his wife erected a memorial on the north wall of the chancel. She also arranged for the installation of a new window above the altar as a 'thankoffering' for his life and example. It was dedicated by the Bishop of Norwich at a special service held on 7 November 1932. It is a beautiful window, described by Pevsner as 'a very good Salvator Mundi and smaller Annunciation'. It floods the church in warm yellows and oranges as the sun rises in the tranquillity of the early morning – a fitting symbol of the peace that Robert found at the end of his twelve years of mental suffering.

Chapter 10

A CHARTER OF RURAL FREEDOM

The second half of the nineteenth century saw a shift in the balance of power in the countryside. In 1884 the franchise had been extended to the rural working classes and in 1894 the Local Government Act was passed, which not only established parish and district councils but also allowed women to vote and stand in their elections. Under the terms of the Act, villages with a population of over 300 were automatically permitted to set up a parish council and those with smaller populations could apply to do so on their own initiative.

On 4 December 1894 a meeting was held in Bessingham with Denham Spurrell in the chair, at which Charles Bishop (seconded by Elijah Crane) proposed that 'this meeting apply to the County Council for an order to establish a Parish Council'[151]. The motion was carried. Robert Emery then proposed that Crane receive 5 shillings from the poor rate for the use of a room in his house, Glebe Cottage, for the parish meetings. A month later, in the evening of 5 January 1895, another meeting was held to elect the first councillors. Denham read the nominations: John Flogdell, Robert Painter, Charles Bishop, Robert Emery and Elijah Crane. The five candidates were duly elected to the five council seats. Six days later the council met for the first time at 7.30 in the evening. Denham was unanimously elected chairman and Painter vice-chairman. Edward Gurney Buxton was elected treasurer and Walter Frankland clerk to the parish council. The rates were set at 2d in the pound, and the clerk's salary was to be £4. It was not long before the perennial problem of road conditions appeared on the agenda. In 1896 the council wrote to Donald Drane* asking him to repair the lane to North Barningham called Little Brig Lane and to Richard Spurrell asking him to repair the lane to Sustead. A few years later Denham himself was asked by Borrett and Emery to 'do something about the Little Brig Lane'[152].

John Borrett had replaced Elijah Crane on the council in 1896 and in 1901 Denham Spurrell and Alfred Grix were elected. The meetings were sometimes held at the Manor House and sometimes at Manor Farm, where in 1904 Walter Frankland's wife Adela was paid 5 shillings for the use of a room. That year it was decided to dissolve the parish council and replace it with a series of parish meetings. Bessingham's first experiment in democracy had been scaled back.

By 1914 the roads were still in poor condition. Appeals to landowners and their agents had had no effect so it was decided to write to Erpingham Rural District Council, 'calling their attention to the dilapidated and dangerous state of the bridle path between the top of Sustead Lane and its junction with the Thurgarton and

---

* Drane was the land agent for the Hanworth Hall estate, which then owned Manor Farm, the cottages at Little Brig and most of the land in North Barningham further down the lane. He was also Denham's distant cousin.

Gresham Road and requesting them to use their authority to have the same placed in proper repair; also to request them to draw the attention of their Surveyor to the condition of the junction of Little Brig Lane with the road known as The Street in Bessingham'[153].

John Tuck attended the parish meetings and after the First World War was involved with an event that was extremely poignant for him. In April 1917 his only son, 23-year-old Charles John Tuck, who was serving with the Egyptian Expeditionary Force, was reported missing after the Battle of Gaza. He was one of two people from Bessingham killed in the war. Herbert Ernest Roper, a private in the Royal Sussex Regiment, also lost his life, dying of his wounds six days before the Armistice. Tuck's loss was all the more tragic in light of the events of his childhood (see Chapter 6). On 14 July 1919 he attended a parish meeting at which Denham proposed that a tablet be erected in the church in memory of the two men who had died serving King and country. Rawlings opposed the plan, saying that the memorial should be in the centre of the village, but Denham's proposal was carried. A committee was thus set up to collect subscriptions and discuss arrangements, made up of Mary Anne Tuck and Mr. Roper (as parents of the deceased), as well as the Rev. E. H. Taylor, Denham Spurrell, Ted Mann, Adela Frankland and Mrs. Brundall.

The war memorial was unveiled during a service held at the church at 3 pm on Sunday, 5 June 1921. Taylor had previously written to the Rev. W. Cass, the United Methodist Minister at Sheringham, with a 'sincere wish' that Cass preach at the service[154]. He had asked on personal grounds, on religious grounds ('it is time we had done with all the bitterness that exists between

Church and Dissent') as well as on social grounds, having previously heard Cass speak on 'our Labour platform'. Taylor's socialism had not endeared him to the local gentry. He was both Rector of Bessingham and Vicar of Sustead, and Richard Spurrell of Thurgarton House, whose family usually worshipped at Sustead, chose to trek across the fields to Thurgarton church to avoid Taylor's sermons at Sustead. Taylor told Cass that he had been attacked by the 'employer and landlord class' because of his claims that the Church of England was 'friends of the rich and not the poor,' giving this as an explanation as to why the churches were empty. 'Half starving' clergy dared not offend the landlords, he wrote, but Taylor challenged them to come out on the side of the people. 'The Working Classes will no longer tolerate the teaching that they are to bow down in subjection to their so-called superiors. I preach Equality and Brotherhood'. Cass accepted the invitation to preach at the service in Bessingham and delivered a sermon entitled 'The Social Needs of the Age'[155].

Erpingham Rural District Council had also been established by the 1894 Local Government Act and Denham was elected to it as the representative for Bessingham. In the year ending March 1896 he attended fourteen of its sixteen meetings, as well as twenty-four of the twenty-six meetings of the Board of Guardians. He also served on the Highways Committee and the Finance Committee at various times.

In 1900 he was sworn in as a Justice of the Peace, sitting on the Cromer bench for the next five decades. I have only found two examples of cases he presided over. In 1904 he and Francis Barclay J.P., brother of Col. Barclay of Hanworth Hall, convicted Albert Higgs of 'unlawfully [driving] a certain motor car recklessly on a certain public highway in the parish of Sheringham, in the county of Norfolk'[156]. The magistrates fined Higgs £10 plus costs, and ordered his licence to be endorsed. One wonders if Denham remembered this when he too was convicted of dangerous driving in Sheringham some forty years later. In Higgs's case, however, the conviction was quashed by the Norfolk Quarter Sessions following an appeal.

The second case took place during the First World War when Denham was one of the magistrates at the Cromer Petty Sessions who fined eighteen fishermen £5 each for failing to report and deliver a wreckage to the Receiver of Wreck – an oversight that was especially serious since Britain was at war.

~

On 17 December 1894 the voters of nearby Aylmerton went to the ballot to elect the village's first ever representative on Erpingham Rural District Council. It was a two-horse race: Denham's sister Emily Mills or the trade unionist and future M.P. George Edwards.

Edwards had been born in Marsham in 1850, the youngest in a family of seven. After his father was gaoled for stealing turnips the family spent time in the workhouse and in 1856 Edwards got his first job scaring crows, earning a shilling a week. He later learned skilled farm work and moved around from job to job. In 1869, he wrote in his autobiography *From Crow-Scaring to Westminster*, he 'obtained work for the summer on a brickfield at Bessingham'[157]. That was the summer when Daniel Spurrell had ordered several thousand bricks, so it is possible that Edwards played a very small role in the construction of Bessingham Manor House. In 1892 he fought his first political campaign for a seat on Norfolk County Council, losing to Benjamin Bond Cabbell by 505 votes to 455. Two years later he sought election again, this time to the district council.

In December 1894 a meeting was held in Aylmerton to discuss the 1894 Local Government Act. Edwards later recalled that the Rector, the Rev. W. W. Mills,

caused some little amusement by his constant personal interjections. For some years for some reason he had shown a personal dislike to me, and he never lost an opportunity to manifest this spirit of dislike. What influenced him I never could understand, but he always seemed jealous of my influence in the village as a Nonconformist. A few days after this meeting was held the Rector came to my house to inform me that Mrs. Mills was being nominated as a candidate for the District Council, and I informed him that I was also being nominated. He expressed a wish that the contest might be friendly. I informed him that so far as I was concerned it would. He then accused me of being the cause of the meeting referred to above being disorderly, which I stoutly denied. He then called me a liar, and it looked for a few moments as if we were in for a scuffle, for I threatened to put him out of my house and began to take steps to do so. He at once rose from his seat and rushed to the door before I could lay hands on him, but in getting away he caught my hand in the door and knocked the skin off my knuckles. My wife was in the next room, and had she not appeared on the scene I do not know what would have happened. She got between us, took the Rector by the collar and put him out of the yard. This event caused some little excitement in the village[158].

Emily Fanny Spurrell and the Rev. William Woodward Mills, long before their marriage in 1879 and their subsequent involvement in Aylmerton politics.

In her election pamphlet Emily pledged to 'brighten the lot of the poor and suffering,'[159] especially children and the elderly. She wanted to change the rules at the workhouse, allowing elderly couples to live together, and she wanted workhouse schools abolished so that the children could attend the local schools. She also proposed that the state provide two-room cottages free of charge to couples who were past working age*.

The Rev. Henry Griffith wrote from Smallburgh Rectory two days after the vote saying he was sorry to hear the people had rejected her. He hoped she would stand again as 'we want ladies on our district councils'[160]. Samuel Groom, the schoolmaster, wrote to William saying he was sorry that Emily was 'not entirely successful'[161]. She had lost by 29 votes to 22.

Despite her service in the village as the rector's wife and her election promises – including the state provision of cottages, which sounds as if it should have come from her opponent's mouth – Edwards had successfully clothed the election in the language of class war.

A letter sent to but rejected by *The Daily Press* by 'GSL' after the 'much talked of election' was over refuted the claim that Emily 'is very seldom seen in the parish' and 'has never been known to take any part in any movement for the benefit of the working class[162]. The writer said that nobody who went to Emily for help was turned away and that George Edwards had done nothing for the labourers in the village.

In January 1895 Edwards wrote to the newspaper saying that before working men got the vote the Church did very little for them. He added that 'every workingman in the village is now fully convinced Mrs. Mills was not brought against me in the interest of labour, but to please one or two of the big farmers'[163]. In another

---

* State pensions were not provided until 1908.

139

letter (this was the golden age of the local newspaper, in which battles were fought in letters to the editor) he said that the working classes now had a chance to be involved in local affairs, calling the Local Government Act a 'charter of rural freedom'[164].

The next election in 1896 was a rerun of Mills versus Edwards, but this time it was Emily's husband who was the candidate. He promised to make changes to poor relief in Aylmerton and manage the road funds better, mending the road past the village school instead of the Lion's Mouth, which was not used as frequently. In April 1896 he contested a letter calling him a 'strong Tory,' claiming he had never acted politically[165]. He narrowly won the election by 31 votes to 29.

~

Since the 1870s elections had been held for the local school boards. In 1898 the Rev. E. H. Taylor, Rector of Bessingham, stood for election to the Aylmerton School Board, pledging religious freedom for board members, the examination of schoolchildren by Church and dissenting ministers in alternate years, the admission of journalists and the public to school board meetings, and a salary for the clerk. The new board, made up of W. W. Mills, E. H. Taylor, Robert Ketton, George Edwards and A. Jolly, met for the first time on 22 October 1898 and Mills was elected chairman. Taylor immediately made a point of order about Samuel Groom's decision to step down as the organist at Sustead church: 'I know why he left, but my information is privileged,' he said, adding that Groom had not been intimidated on religious grounds[166]. Edwards, who had previously claimed that the Church was not on the side of the working man, now found an unlikely ally in the Rev. E. H. Taylor, who later declared that he had been elected to the school board 'as the representative of the working classes'[167]. Taylor proposed (seconded by Edwards) to move the board meetings from 5 pm to 8 pm so that working men could attend. Mills and Ketton said that the late hour was 'inconvenient,' although Ketton, more of a pragmatist than Mills, 'doubted if the public would take the trouble to come' even if the time were changed. Edwards and Taylor insisted that 'personal convenience' should not come before 'public duty'. The motion was defeated, as were Taylor's proposals for alternating religious examination and giving the clerk a salary. Finally, Mills said that Taylor's motion that the schoolmaster be free to attend whichever place of worship he likes was 'an insult to me,' adding 'I refuse to put it'. Edwards replied that 'it is really most extraordinary conduct for you to refuse to put it. A legitimate resolution ought to be put. I will second Mr. Taylor's motion'. Taylor said that the public's distrust of the board would only be intensified if the motion was not put and Mills vehemently replied 'I don't care for the public; the public may draw what inferences it likes. I won't allow such a resolution to be put; it is a direct insult'.

The following month *The Cromer and North Walsham Post* reported that Mills had intimidated Groom, asking him not to attend church services at Sustead. Taylor revealed that 'Mr. Denham Spurrell (a gentleman well known and highly respected throughout the district) told Groom, "Mrs. Mills has very great respect for you, and if you wish to retain it you had better leave Sustead Church"'[168]. Yet Groom insisted that Mills had never 'threatened, coerced, or intimidated him'. In a letter to the *Cromer and North Walsham Post* on 5 November 1898 Mills sought to clarify matters, stating that Groom had been an excellent and respected schoolmaster for thirteen years. Groom wrote the same day saying he did not know why Taylor had to bring up the matter of his decision to leave Sustead, saying his work there as an organist, as well as his choir and committee work, had always been greatly appreciated. The reasons for his departure from Sustead church are never clearly stated in the letters or board meeting reports that Mills cut out from the newspapers and pasted into his scrapbook, but Taylor knew that Groom did not approve of certain practices at Sustead and it was probably a case of Groom seeking a church where he felt more at home with the style of worship. Emily may have spoken to him and this may have influenced his decision to leave, but he could have been contemplating a change anyway. Whatever the truth, it is clear that Taylor and Edwards used it as a means to attack Mills, despite Edwards's later protests that 'it was unfair to infer that a league existed between Mr. Taylor and himself to attack the chairman'[169].

The issue rolled on into 1899 when in January a letter to the *Cromer and North Walsham Post* from 'An Exposer' criticised Taylor for not addressing educational matters but for using the board meetings as a platform from which to launch attacks on Mills. 'The performance has a generally pantomimic character'[170]. The writer thought Taylor did not represent the working classes but was rather the 'personification of antipathy to the chairman'. The public quarrel reached new heights in February 1899 when Taylor accused Mills of knowingly allowing a teacher to come to Sunday school who had been found 'defiling boys with immorality' elsewhere[171].

Mills's scrapbook ends there and no more is known of these public disagreements. Mills continued to serve as Rector of Aylmerton-cum-Runton until he retired in 1915 after 43 years at the age of 84. Taylor was Rector of Bessingham and Vicar of Sustead until his death in 1947 at the age of 83, having served the two parishes for a remarkable 51 years. Edwards was re-elected to Erpingham Rural District Council in 1897 and served as chairman of the sanitary committee before leaving North Norfolk. He later became a magistrate and was awarded an O.B.E. for his work on various committees during the First World War. In 1920 he was elected M.P. for South Norfolk, representing the constituency until 1922 and again from 1923 to 1924. He was knighted in 1930 and died in 1933 at the age of 83.

Chapter 11

DESERTERS FROM THE PLOUGH

Britain's population had increased from 7.5 million in 1781 to 26 million in 1881 and those extra mouths needed to be fed, and cheaply too. Farmers had increased output accordingly but in the 1870s the market found another solution. Huge quantities of cheap grain from North America (where farming was entering a golden age after the end of the Civil War and the arrival of the railways in the West) began to flood the British market. Coupled with a series of bad harvests, this triggered a period of agricultural depression in the closing decades of the nineteenth century. Wheat prices halved in England between the 1870s and 1890s. Arable land was turned into permanent pasture, which was less labour-intensive.

'On the good wheatlands of Norfolk the impact of the depression was ... not as serious as many believed'[172]. Nevertheless, wages, rents and production all fell, and as always, it was the poor who were hit the hardest. Many left the countryside to seek new opportunities in the growing towns and cities, where employers found them to be stronger and in better health than their urban counterparts. Bessingham's population fell from 151 in 1871 to 125 in 1891. A look at the censuses shows that Bessingham's 'deserters from the plough' were living not only in other parts of Norfolk but also in London and some of the industrial cities of the north. William Shepherd, for example, was a labourer on a shipyard in Hartlepool in 1891; James Corbyn was a bus conductor in London; and 86-year-old James Clark had moved to Doncaster to be with his grandson.

A note in one of the labour account books refers to a decision taken on 15 September 1894:

> At a meeting of the Members of the Farmers Federation held today at N. Walsham it was unanimously resolved that in consequence of the recent ruinous fall in value of all kinds of corn the current rate of wages be reduced to ten shillings a week as soon as soon as (sic) usual notice can take effect after harvest[173].

Wages fell steadily during the 1880s and 1890s. By November 1900 they were between fifteen and seventeen shillings a fortnight and by the following April the highest wage was 14s 6d. The 1895 harvest began on 3 August and Daniel negotiated wages of between £4 10s and £6 5s – much lower than the peak of £8 in 1875 – and told the men they could have all the rabbits they found in the corn. On 8 August they killed about thirty rabbits. They worked long days. On 5 August they were in the fields from 5.40 am to 9.30 pm. The threshing machine arrived after breakfast on 21 August and 33 cwt of oats from Gresham were threshed that day as well as 23 cwt of barley from Lords Lands and Great Croft.

A few days after the harvest ended in 1897, 12-year-old William Randall was sitting on a horse that was pulling a corn reaper driven by Alfred Crow. The horse suddenly took fright and William fell backwards onto the reaper. Alfred was thrown from his seat too but fell clear of the knives. One of William's arms and one of his legs were cut off and his skull was fractured. Daniel noted in his account book that William was 'so much cut that he died within 5 hours'[174].

In October 1900 there were fifteen men and boys on the books. John Tuck, George Green, Alfred Grix, Robert Bumphrey and James Corbyn were all working in the garden and Alfred Crowe, Ben Aldridge, John Claxton, Harry Crowe, George Jones, Fred King, Bob Green, Robert Hall, Charley Randall and the boy Smith were ploughing, thrashing, carting turnips, drilling wheat, feeding bullocks, carting muck and cleaning swedes and mangels. The boy Smith earned three shillings and the men received no more than 14s 6d.

Rents also fell, and this was noticed most on large estates that were divided into tenant farms, such as Holkham along the coast, where rents in the 1890s were half what they had been in the 1870s. Although Bessingham was run as a single entity, Billockby Hall and Flaxman's Farm were let to tenant farmers, and even as late as the 1930s Flaxman's Farm was being let for £85 18s per annum, less than half the amount that John Clark had paid in 1869. But the Bessingham estate managed to remain intact. 'Many gentleman farmers survived especially in areas like north Norfolk, and parts of Lincolnshire, Yorkshire, and Northumberland where economies of scale protected the cereal farmer'[175]. Landowners were not indifferent to their tenants' calls to reduce rents – indeed they would rather receive lower rents than see the farm stand idle.

Between 1910 and 1915 an extensive survey of Britain's farmland was conducted by the Land Valuation office. The survey was brought about as the result of Lloyd George's so-called People's Budget, which introduced a capital gains tax on the value of land when it was sold. The maps and field books that make up the survey are extremely useful to local historians since they provide detailed information about the ownership and occupation of land and houses, including the rental and market values. The groundwork for the Bessingham field books was done by Guy Davey, who lived at Sustead Old Hall and was the agent for Col. Barclay of Hanworth Hall and Sir Samuel Hoare of Sidestrand Hall. He provided the inventory of land and buildings so that the government inspector could carry out the valuations.

Bessingham Manor House, with its outbuildings and 335 acres of land, was assessed at a market value of £10,450, excluding sporting rights of £670 and timber valued at £400. The house was considered to be in excellent condition. The outbuildings included eleven cowhouses, five piggeries, a calf house, bullock lodges, bullock boxes, an implement house, a copper house, a chaff house, a turnip shed, a stable for nine horses, and a six-bay cart shed with a granary above.

Most of the villagers paid about £5 a year for a two-up, two-down cottage built of brick, flint and pantiles. John Tuck's cottage (now called Tall Chimneys) contained three rooms on each floor and was let for £6, its market value being £76. John Flogdell also paid £6 a year for his cottage, which had a shop, kitchen and living room on the ground floor and three bedrooms above. The pub, which was worth £700, was let to John Eglington. It was a brick, flint and pantile building with five bedrooms, a taproom, bar, cellar, living room, scullery, stable, cart shed, garden and 1 acre of land. Walter Frankland owned Church Cottages, which have his ancestor's initials GF on the wall facing the road. Reginald Batt of Gresham owned the two cottages at Little Brig, valued at £45 and £50, one of which was rented by the Malletts for £4 a year. He also owned Manor Farm and 41 acres of land, 'a good little farm, the arable and pasture are quite above the average and appears to have been well kept up. The house and buildings are in very fair repair'[176]. It was let to Walter Frankland for £54 per year and valued at £834.

The twentieth century also brought in more regulations for farmers. In 1906 Denham Spurrell fell foul of regulations regarding the fat content in milk and was summoned to appear before the magistrates for allegedly selling adulterated milk[*]. Samples were taken and the fat content was found to be 2.79 per cent, whereas genuine milk was said to contain no less than 3 per cent. It was decided, however, that the 'lowering in the fat percentage' was due to 'the jolting the milk would undergo in being taken about the town'[177]. The unusual weather at the time was also considered a factor and the case was dismissed.

During the First World War imports fell and demand increased for home-grown cereals. Prices rose accordingly and land was once again seen as a stable investment. After the war the government pledged to continue supporting agriculture and many landowners, realising that they would probably never have another

---

[*] There seem to be as many reports of him appearing before the magistrates as there are of him sitting on the bench.

opportunity as good as this, decided to sell some of their land. 1919 saw the biggest transfer of land in Britain in almost a thousand years. Most of the buyers were sitting tenants and the hand-over was smooth. Denham tried to sell Flaxman's Farm in 1923, which had been valued at £1,955 during the 1910-1915 valuation, but he had missed the boat. The Agricultural Act that kept prices stable during the war was repealed in 1921 and farming was once again entering hard times.

Around the country many of the labourers who had left to fight in the Great War did not want to return to the land. In January 1914, a few months before the lamps went out all over Europe, there were twenty names on the books: C. and J. Doy, Bishop, Hudson, G. and R. Green, Williamson, Lightwing, H. and C. Roper, Pye, Gotts, Jones, Bumfrey, Tuck, Flogdell, King, A. and S. Gotts and Cooper. They all earned 14 to 16 shillings. The following March there were seventeen men and in February 1919 only thirteen: Mann, Starling, Black, Green, Flogdell, Stearman, Spendloff, Shepherd, Finch, Tuck, Flogdell and F. and T. Curtis.

Farmers sought to compensate for these changes by introducing new crops to update the traditional model of wheat, barley, turnips and grass. The first sugar beet factory in Britain was opened in 1921 at Cantley on the Broads, and peas and potatoes also began to be grown in increasing numbers, including in Bessingham. Marketing Boards were set up in the 1930s to protect food producers and guarantee minimum prices, the Milk Marketing Board being the most successful and best remembered.

~

In 1928 Denham turned seventy and decided to stop managing the estate as a single entity. There were eleven men on the books in the final months of that year: John Bishop, W. Bishop, Foster Lawrence, Cecil Blake, George Loynes, James Culley, Reggie Bishop, Albert Finch, George Green, W. Bacon and W. Ling, earning between £1 10s and £1 15 6d in wages. Bacon, who was milking on most days, received the highest wage in October 1928. The others were spreading muck, mending the stables, cleaning the tower and driveway or driving the water cart and turnip cart. The following month they were also ringing pigs, catching moles, pruning trees and sowing wheat. Two casual workers were hired in December for a few days' work: Cooper to mend a wagon and other things, and Shales to repair the copper and water troughs and put up tiles. The same month Horace Wright paid Denham £88 8s for several cows, pigs, rabbits and sheep fleeces, and the following year he began renting Manor House Farm and 450 acres of land from Denham for £462 per year.

In 1940 and 1941 the government inspected farms around the country to see how they were contributing to the war effort, and between 1941 and 1943 they carried out further surveys for post-war planning. Together these are known as the National Farm Survey. In 1941, according to the survey, Horace grew 115 acres of wheat, 57 acres of oats and 16 acres of sugar beet at Manor House Farm. He also had two acres of kale – now a trendy superfood but then grown as fodder for animals – as well as beans, peas, turnips and mangels, all of which were also fed to his livestock. He had 53 cattle, 110 sheep, 28 pigs, 129 poultry and 15 horses. For the 1941 harvest he had ploughed up 57 acres of grassland in Bessingham and sown oats and wheat as part of the war effort. The inspector graded farms according to their productivity and use of modern farming methods. The inspector found Horace old-fashioned in his ways, despite having a 'petrol engine' and two 25 horsepower Fordson tractors, and said that the farm could be improved by someone with a better knowledge of fertilisers. He gave Horace a B.

Detail from the 1946 aerial map of Norfolk, showing Manor House Farm (centre), then occupied by Horace Wright. The walled garden is to the east and the Manor House is screened from the road by trees. Glebe (now Rectory) Cottage is in the bottom left and other cottages can be seen along The Street.

Horace's son Granville and his daughter-in-law Hilda rented The Den for £40 a year from 1939. There were fourteen acres on which Granville grew wheat, oats, potatoes and grass, and he also kept 22 pigs, 161 chickens and 4 horses. The inspector was impressed with the farm and gave it an A.

The Den, photographed in 1973. Originally a pair of labourer's cottages, it was enlarged in the early 1900s for Flaxman C. J. Spurrell; later occupants included Catherine O'Connell and Granville and Hilda Wright.

S. G. Bumphrey rented Manor Farm from the Batts for £52 10s a year, growing barley, wheat, oats, turnips and grass. The farm had no electricity and was infested with wood pigeons and rooks. The inspector found that Bumphrey lacked knowledge of modern methods and the farm was therefore given a B.

Some of the land in Bessingham belonged to Thurgarton Hall, which was leased from the Felbrigg estate for £417 5s a year. It was considered a grade A farm and had electricity as well as four 'petrol engines' and one tractor. William Donald, the farmer, also occupied twenty-six acres of Hanworth common, which he ploughed up for the 1941 harvest and sowed mostly with oats.

The work of increasing agricultural production during the Second World War was given to government-supported organisations called War Agricultural Executive Committees, or 'War Ags'. Cecil Blake, who had worked in the gardens of Bessingham Manor House in the 1930s, and Fred Hudson, who lived at Glebe Cottage, carried out work for the 'War Ag', draining land in Gresham so that it could be cultivated. Another development brought about by the war was the arrival of German and Italian prisoners of war. Based at Matlaske, they helped both Horace and Granville Wright on their farms and were on friendly terms with the local population. Granville liked to test the local ales on the German POWs, who were used to lighter lagers back home. His wife Hilda continued to correspond with one POW after the war and even visited him in Heidelberg. There were also evacuees in the village: the Wisemans took in two sisters, for example.

As Jock Lane recalls of his short time in North Norfolk in the early 1950s, farming was far from being fully mechanised. Sugar beet was still hoed by hand and harvesting involved a lot of horses and manual work before modern combine harvesters took over.

~

In 1931 Denham's niece Sybil Hitchcock left her job as an art teacher at Sandecotes School in Dorset and moved to Bessingham Manor House with her recently widowed mother. Two years later Sybil married Francis Gordon

Haward, a Suffolk farmer, and for the next ten years they rented Thurgarton House from Denham's cousin George Spurrell. George had inherited the estate on his father's death in 1933 but he was only in his twenties and sought adventure elsewhere. He went to Africa, where he worked as a colonial administrator and pig farmer in the Gold Coast (now Ghana) for about fifteen years. Joy Wright and Joyce Mallet, who both grew up in Bessingham in the 1930s, remember the Christmas parties thrown by Sybil and Francis for children from the village. Francis dressed up as Father Christmas and handed out presents. On 2 July 1943 he died at Thurgarton House and Sybil moved to Hampshire. While the Hawards were living in the house it was another distant cousin, Thomas Henry Dix of Swannington, who acted as George's land agent until he returned from Africa. The government inspector described Dix as a 'spare time farmer' and noted that he 'fails to give the farm the attention that he should'[178]. He found the farm lanes (including the one that brothers William and John Spurrell were arguing about in 1816 and the parish council was discussing in more recent decades) in a 'bad' condition. The classification was B. The 405 acre estate was mostly arable, with a small amount of grassland. It included 140 acres of land in neighbouring Sustead, as well as Sustead Old Hall, which had been purchased by George's grandfather in about 1888 from the trustees of John Ketton of Felbrigg Hall.

Chapter 12

A HAPPY VILLAGE

Many of those who stayed in Bessingham during the depression years of the late nineteenth century found alternative work to make ends meet. The 1891 census lists about a dozen occupations in addition to farmer and labourer: groom, gardener, farm steward, blacksmith, carpenter, bricklayer, joiner, painter, grocer, dressmaker, laundress and shoemaker. There were also three maids at the Manor House, all aged between 16 and 21. The farmers in the village, in addition to Daniel and now Denham Spurrell, were William Cooper at The Den, Elijah Crane at Glebe Farm and Philip Woods at Manor Farm. The old Manor House, called 'Old House' on the census, was still in occupation. According to village lore, it burned down, although I have so far been unable to determine if or when this happened. It was obviously still habitable in 1891, when John Tuck was living there with his wife and children, so the fire must have occurred later on. By 1901 John had moved to The Street, where he was living in the cottage now known as Tall Chimneys. His wife Mary Anne was the postmistress and his daughter Margery collected the letters.

The 1911 census lists twenty-nine occupied houses:

Head of household	Address	No. of rooms
John Eglington	Horse Shoes Inn	7
Flaxman Spurrell	The Den	10
Denham Spurrell	Manor House	18
Thomas Fish	New Road	5
George Green	The Street	4
John Flogdell	The Street	4
Sarah Leeder	The Clematis	4
Hannah Bricknell	The Ivy	4
Eliza Frankland	Church House	4
George Farrow	The Street	5
John Tuck	The Street	5
Charles Randell	The Street	4
Benjamin Farrow	The Street	3
James Thompson	The Street	4
Robert Neale	The Street	5
Frederick King	The Street	4
George Jones	The Street	4
William Bowery	The Street	4
Harriet Spettigue	Glebe Cottage	4
John Flogdell	The Street	3
James Bacon	Bessingham	4
Dennis Mallett	Bessingham	4
John Goldspink	Bessingham	4
Dennis Bishop	Bessingham	5
Charles Cooper	Bessingham	5
Walter Frankland	Manor Farm	6
William Strong	Little Brig Lane	4
Robert Massingham	Little Brig Lane	4
George Thaxter	Bessingham	5

Denham lived at the Manor House with his sister Kitty and three female servants, all aged between 20 and 25. Kitty's cousin Flaxman, whom she had not yet married, was living at The Den with an attendant and a housekeeper, who were husband and wife. The addresses on the census are short and not altogether enlightening, but by working out the census enumerator's route it is possible to identify some of the houses. Thomas Fish, whose address is given as New Road, lived at Manor House Farm and was employed as Denham's farm bailiff. George Green and John Flogdell lived in the pair of cottages that are now Pestle Cottage. Sarah Leeder, Hannah Bricknell and Eliza Frankland are all occupying the cottages belonging to Walter Frankland now called Church Cottages. The enumerator continued down The Street, reaching Glebe Cottage where Harriet Spettigue, a Cornish lady who in 1898 had published a novel called *The Heritage of Eve*, resided with her niece. The houses for which the address is given only as 'Bessingham' are on the lane leading to Manor Farm.

After Kitty Spurrell died in 1919 The Den was let to various people. William Ingram Cooke, a private tutor, lived there in 1929, and in the next decade it was the home of Catherine O'Connell, the widow of an army tutor. The O'Connells had rented Sustead Old Hall from Denham's cousin in the early 1900s and had also spent time in Cromer. Catherine was joined at The Den for a short while by her son and daughter-in-law and their two children, Patrick and Shelagh O'Connell. The O'Connells left The Den when Shelagh was still a baby, but stories of their time have left an impression on her. While transcribing the Bessingham parish registers for the

Norfolk Family History Society in 2012* I came across the baptisms of Shelagh and Patrick. Thanks to various internet sources I was able to discover that Shelagh was then serving as Chairman of Norfolk County Council. Several emails followed in which she told me more about her family's links with North Norfolk and in a few cases I was able to provide some context based on the research I had done.

~

Alfred Blake speaks for many of the people who grew up in Bessingham in the interwar years, recalling a 'happy and carefree' place where the people were 'very kind'[179]. His father Cecil had moved to Bessingham after the First World War, working in the gardens of the Manor House and also as the village gravedigger. Cecil's father had been a gamekeeper on the Barningham estate and also worked as a part-time gamekeeper in Bessingham in the early twentieth century when Denham still hosted shooting parties.

Many people would agree with Alfred's statement that 'Bessingham was a happy village'[180]. George Finch remembers running along the lanes with hoops made from old bicycle wheels with the spokes taken out, or wandering freely across the cattle meadows by the beck. Joy Wright speaks of roaming through the grounds of the Manor House too, and according to Nell and Gill Hudson the children were able to play everywhere except on the manicured bowls lawn.

---

* An exercise I thought would be useful in helping me follow the names of Bessingham families over the generations.

The gardens were 'immaculate'[181] under Denham thanks to the hard work of George Green, the head gardener (probably the son of the 'turnip boy' on the 1851 census). The walled garden, where Denham's sister had grown row upon row of bulbs, served as the kitchen garden. It was entered through a gate by the old coach house and laid out with grass paths. Espaliered fruit trees grew along the north wall. Nell Hudson and Joy Wright remember apples, pears, peaches and medlars. There were also redcurrant and whitecurrant bushes, raspberry cages and a prized asparagus bed. It was a 'warm enclosed garden'[182], says Joy, and while Denham was at market on Saturday morning some of the children would go scrumping for fruit.

Another reliable presence in the gardens was Maurice Wiseman. Born in Essex, he met his wife Ruby while she was in service there but they decided to move back to her native Norfolk after her employer died. Maurice found work with East Coast Motors in Cromer but in about 1929 heard that a man was needed for a few weeks at Bessingham. He was hired and ended up staying for forty years. He was a kind man and became a valued and trusted employee not only of Denham but also of his successor Ronald Hitchcock, for whom he almost singlehandedly took care of the Manor House and grounds in the 1950s and 1960s. Maurice looked after the lawns and conservatory, tended to the beehives, and was also a chauffeur and handyman, making repairs to the cottages when needed. The conservatory contained maidenhair ferns and primula obonica plants, which Nell Hudson would water for Denham, as well as a large camellia tree. Mary Willcox (née Ives) remembers

Denham bringing camellia flowers to her parents at Erpingham House whenever he visited.

Bessingham Manor House photographed by my grandfather Charles Spurrell in the 1930s. My grandmother Mildred can be seen on the right next to the conservatory. Their car is parked under the porte-cochère.

Every year the grounds of the Manor House were thrown open for the village fete. Olive Hudson was part of a small committee of volunteers who helped to organise it. There were cakes and ice creams, competitions and raffles, and the children wore fancy dress. Olive's daughter Nell went as Britannia one year, with a hat made from newspaper and painted gold. The Manor House also hosted sports days for Gresham village school. One year the Countess of Orford, whose father, the Rev. T. H. R. Oakes, was Rector of Thurgarton in the 1930s, presented the prizes and the children were taken home at 9 pm in farm waggons.

Another event that was celebrated with a party at the Manor House was the multiple christening of 1932. Fourteen children (one Lawrence, two Malletts, four Bishops, four Fieldses and three Wrights) were baptised on 16 October by the Rev. E. H. Taylor. Joy Wright was one of those christened that day and said that the rector had rounded up all the unbaptised children in the village and her grandfather Horace stood as godfather to several of them. Joyce Mallett remembers the rector as a 'dear old man'[183] whose unfortunate facial expressions sometimes made her and the other children giggle. The Malletts usually attended the Methodist chapel, where Timothy Rounce preached until it closed in the early 1950s, but attended the village church for special occasions such as the harvest festival. They had also donated to the church organist fund in 1919, along with the Franklands, Tucks, Manns, Flogdells, Denham Spurrell, and local dignitaries such as the Earl of Orford, Douglas King (the M.P. for North Norfolk) and the Barclay family. In his letter seeking donations Taylor wrote that Bessingham 'is a very poor parish near Cromer, as you know. But nor do we want the services of our church to suffer through a want of money'[184]. The church had a thriving choir at this time as well as a Sunday school taught by Adela Frankland. When he first arrived at Bessingham, Taylor had sought to bring the Church closer to the people. In addition to the three services offered at the church on Sundays (Holy Communion at 8 am and Morning Prayer at 11 am, and Evensong every other week at 6 pm), as well as Evensong at 7.30 pm on Wednesdays and Fridays, he led 'cottage services'[185] at 3.15 pm on Wednesdays and 8 pm on Fridays, which featured hymns, prayers, Bible readings and a short homily. The parish magazine reported that the cottage services were well attended.

The Rev. E. H. Taylor with members of the church choir in 1920. Taylor was Rector of Bessingham and Vicar of Sustead from 1896 until his death in 1947.

Sunday school members photographed in 1920, many sitting or standing on Spurrell tombs.

For the men in the village the pub offered a place to socialise and relax, as it had done for generations. During the Second World War it was also where the Home Guard met. According to Joy Wright, people in the village always knew where to find them – either at the Horse Shoes Inn or at the Black Boys in Aldborough. The publican at this time was Ted Mann, who had taken over the licence from Emma Eglington in 1918. Emma had run the pub with her husband since 1900 and continued to do so for a few years after his death in 1914. She was the daughter of Isaac Mallett, who had worked as an agricultural labourer in Thurgarton and later settled in Bessingham. Emma's nephew Albert Isaac Mallett joined her in Bessingham in about 1920, working as a cobbler while his wife ran a small shop in the front room of their home at Yew Tree Cottage. They also rented a field from Denham on which they kept a horse.

Albert Mallett with his sister Ethel, daughter Joyce and a pig in the field behind Yew Tree Cottage in the 1930s.

Joyce Mallett (left) outside Yew Tree Cottage and (right) with
her sisters Queenie and Christine Mallett.

The Malletts had pigs, rabbits, goats, turkeys, geese
and bees too, and grew a lot of vegetables and fruit. They
made fruit wine and also ate pheasants and other game
that had been poached. According to their daughter
Joyce, their rent for the cottage, garden and field was £7
per year in the 1930s. The cottages in Bessingham were
generally in good repair and spacious, Joyce recalls. Each
had an immaculate garden, with flowers along the path,
and vegetables and sometimes chickens in the garden.

Albert and Rosa Finch lived at Rose Cottage, which
was later renamed Finch Cottage. Albert came from
Northamptonshire but Rosa had grown up in the village
– her father John Borrett had served on the parish council
in the late 1890s while living at Little Brig. Albert and
Rosa had five children: Lorna, who died at the age of five
after eating deadly nightshade, Agnes and Peggy, who

both worked at the Manor House for a while, and two boys, Ted and George.

Agnes Finch (left) outside the Manor House in the 1930s whilst employed as a housemaid, and George Finch (right).

George remembers Timothy Rounce delivering milk to the house, carrying the churns on the handlebars of his bicycle. George would stand at the front door, holding out a cup that Timothy would fill. A few years later George went to Manor House Farm after school to help Horace Wright with the milking. He also lent a hand to Horace's son Granville at harvest time and remembers Granville's two horses, Nelson and Boxer, who did all the heavy work of ploughing, harrowing and carting. Granville and Hilda Wright had moved into The Den in 1939 after Catherine O'Connell left. The house had no electricity or running water at the time, which was not at all uncommon. Maurice Wiseman came to decorate some of the rooms before they moved in. There were five rooms downstairs and six bedrooms upstairs, accessed by two separate staircases, and lots of bulbs outside – survivors of the 10,000 daffodils that had been planted by Kitty Spurrell. Denham did not like Granville, maybe because he was rather partial to the odd whisky, so the lease for The Den was in Hilda's name, which was to cause a problem for Granville when Hilda died (see Chapter 13).

One of the priorities of Attlee's post-war government was to respond to the housing crisis and between 1945 and 1951 a million new homes were built across the country. Local authorities were given additional powers to achieve this and on 5 March 1949 Erpingham Rural District Council issued a compulsory purchase order for 1.15 acres of land in Bessingham then owned by Denham Spurrell and occupied by the Whites. Four council houses were built and Granville's brother Jack and his wife Gladys were among the first people to move in.

Parents often sent their children to pay their rent at the Manor House. Joy Wright recalls entering via the yard and walking along the passage to Denham's study. To George Finch the Manor House was 'palatial'[186]. He would often visit his sister Peggy there on Saturday mornings when she was in service. Agnes Finch, Florrie Green, Dorothy Mallet, Eleanor Hook and Dorothy Fields were all in service around this time too.

By the 1930s John Tuck was enjoying his retirement. The Manor had been a vital part of his life for as long as he could remember and in 1925 he chose to back a horse called Manna in the Derby. Manna won and John spent his winnings on a tricycle, which he rode to Cromer to do his shopping. He would sometimes leave the tricycle outside garden gates in Bessingham or Gresham and the children would attempt to ride it. According to George Finch, only 'Tuppenny' Pike could do so without falling off.

Long before he bought his tricycle John Tuck would take a horse and trap and go to Cromer to run errands for Denham. One day, so the story goes, Denham made the short journey instead of John and on the way back to Bessingham he was amused to find that the horse came to a stop outside every pub.

PART FIVE

AFTER 1952

Chapter 13

A GHOST VILLAGE

Mention the name Hitchcock in Bessingham even today and people think not of the great film director but of Ronald Victor Hitchcock, the last squire of Bessingham. But he was not the only Hitchcock associated with the village. Both his parents are buried in the churchyard and it was his sister Sybil who threw Christmas parties for children in the 1930s.

Ronald's mother, Mary Isabelle Spurrell, had married Frank George Armstrong Hitchcock in 1882. Frank was the son of George Hitchcock and his second wife Elizabeth Mary Armstrong. George was a wealthy London merchant. He lived at 22 Norfolk Crescent, not far from Hyde Park, and owned a firm of drapers on Cheapside. In 1844 his employee, and later son-in-law, George Williams started organising scripture meetings for workers on the firm's premises. As these meetings grew in popularity they became more structured and out of them the Y.M.C.A. was formed.

Frank Hitchcock was educated at Rugby and Trinity College, Cambridge, and three years after marrying Mary he qualified as a solicitor. He practised for many years at 20 Victoria Street, London, living in West Kensington before moving to the suburbs of South London and then out to Kent. He and Mary had six children: Frank Norman Spurrell (1883), Ronald Victor (1884), Sybil Mary (1886), Gladys Violet (1888), Sylvia Daisy (1889) and Audrey Myrtle (1892). After Frank's death at Portsmouth City Mental Hospital (now St. James's Hospital) in 1930 his widow moved back to her childhood home in Bessingham. A photograph taken by my grandfather shows her standing on the lawn outside the Manor House with Denham and my grandmother Mildred in the 1930s. My Aunt Caroline remembers being taken to Bessingham shortly after the Second World War by my grandfather. She has a clear memory of seeing an old lady lying in bed. She reached out to take one of the sweets on the bedside table, only to be told sternly by the old lady that they were her pills. The old lady was almost certainly Mary. She eventually moved to Vale Lodge in Sheringham, where she died in 1948 at the age of 91.

Mary Isabelle Hitchcock with Denham Spurrell and my grandmother Mildred outside Bessingham Manor House in the 1930s.

When Denham passed away in 1952 it was Mary's son Ronald who inherited the estate passed. Ronald later told the *Daily Mail* that it had been 'nothing but a headache'[187], so why did Denham choose him as his heir? Both Denham and his brother died without issue and of his five sisters only two had children of their own: Emily and Mary. Emily's son Daniel Mills had met with a fatal accident in South Africa in 1904 and her two daughters were spinsters all their lives. Mary had not only six children but also seven grandchildren and by choosing a Hitchcock heir Denham hoped that the estate would remain in the family for years to come. He had other options too. He could have left instructions for the estate to be sold, but the welfare of his tenants must always have been somewhere in the back of his mind and the sale would have been disruptive to the village. Keeping the estate in the family was more important. He could have chosen to leave it to his cousin George Spurrell at Thurgarton House or even another distant relative such as my grandfather, but Ronald was his sister's son and therefore the obvious choice.

I do not know when Ronald first knew that he would inherit the estate. Like all heirs to Bessingham he was not the first-born. His elder brother Frank, a doctor who had emigrated to New Zealand before the First World War, was killed in France in 1916 while serving with the New Zealand Medical Corps. Ronald also spent most of his adult life overseas. He obtained a degree in engineering from King's College London in 1911 and went out to India as an engineer with the Great Indian Peninsula Railway. When he retired in 1939 he returned to England, moving into the family home at Fleet in Hampshire.

Ronald Victor Hitchcock in the 1930s, many years before he became the last squire of Bessingham.

Ronald was almost 70 and unable to drive when he inherited the estate. He decided to be a hands-off squire, intervening as little as possible in village affairs. He came up by train once or twice a year to collect rents, deal with urgent estate business and oversee the raspberry harvest. He took various pieces of furniture, including a baby grand piano, back to Fleet. His wife Beatrice did not look forward to their visits and soon stopped coming. Their grandson Sheridan Hughes, however, spent a few weeks of his summer holidays in Bessingham in the 1960s. The house was already showing signs of its age, and being unoccupied for most of the year did not help. Sheridan remembers the wind whistling through a crack in the front door and decorations that dated from well before the First World War.

~

'The villagers looked on me as a foreigner and were hostile from the start. I hate going there'[188], Ronald told the *Daily Mail* after fourteen years as squire of Bessingham. There were several reasons for this animosity towards the village, which was mutual. One was that, in the eyes of many, the village 'went downhill fast'[189], as Alfred Blake put it. The newspapers were quick to label it a 'ghost village'[190].

Denham, like many landowners whose estates had been in a single family for generations, had kept rents low and carried out repairs to keep the cottages in good shape. In Ronald's opinion, however, the tenants expected more than was reasonable for the rents they paid, so he began to increase them. Albert and Rosa Finch's rent for Rose Cottage was £6 14s in 1939. This did not rise until 1954, when Ronald put it up to £8 0s 11d, followed by a sharp rise to £17 9s 4d four years later. By 1964 it was up to £22 0s 6d and in 1968 it was £25 14s 1d, roughly four times what it had been only fourteen years earlier. But despite the increased rental income Ronald did not always carry out repairs. He allowed many properties to stand empty, even turning down offers to buy or rent them. An empty cottage meant less to worry about. The district council was powerless to do anything about it, and George Spurrell, chairman of Sustead parish council (with which Bessingham parish council had merged), said in 1963: 'As I see it, it is a situation about which nothing can be done – the Parish Council has no power over landlords to make them let their properties, and we have never talked about it. The last time we had a vacancy there was no great rush'[191]. A spokesman for the district council confirmed that they had only one person on their waiting list for Bessingham. Of the village's twelve empty properties in 1963, nine belonged to Ronald.

The pub was another casualty of Ronald's laissez-faire approach. 'For decades [it] echoed to the laughter of its customers, the chink of glasses, the thud of darts'[192], but in 1959 the brewery decided not to renew the licence. So few people drank there that it was not worth paying the rent. For those such as Jack Wright who had still gone for a drink at the Horse Shoes Inn, The Chequers in Gresham was the most convenient alternative. 'If it wasn't for the council houses,' thought Rosemary Shepherd, 'Bessingham would become dead altogether'[193]. 'There's no neighbourliness in Bessingham any more,' said Rosa Finch in 1963, 'because everyone is going away. But my roots are here and I wouldn't want to go. It's not nice for the little children, either – there's three little 'uns here and that's all'[194].

A journalist with the *Eastern Daily Press* managed to get through to Ronald on the phone. Ronald said it was 'quite common' for cottages to be unoccupied but declined to say whether he had received any offers to rent the empty properties. 'You have no business to be doing this,' he told the journalist sharply, 'it is no business of anyone's'[195].

Bessingham's population dropped from 124 to 50 in the fourteen years after Denham's death. Both George Finch and Alfred Blake left in 1965. George got married that year and wanted to be able to buy a house, which was not possible in Bessingham. Some residents were actively chased out by Ronald. When Hilda Wright died in 1963 Ronald took her widower Granville to court and was granted an eviction order because The Den was in her name. Granville duly left the village, moving to Aylmerton where he continued to farm until his retirement, but for Ronald closing up The Den meant having one less thing on his mind.

If we put ourselves in Ronald's shoes – retired, unable to drive, and living a long way from an estate that demanded a great deal of correspondence and energy to run – we can begin to understand why he wanted to make things as simple as he could. He claimed to be doing what he thought would be best for his family when he was gone, but to those in the village who had always enjoyed a close relationship with their squire, Ronald's insistence on not interfering made him seem aloof and indifferent. The Rev. Cyril Pegler obviously went too far in saying that Ronald wanted to see the village die, but he certainly wanted to reduce his dealings with it to a more manageable level. One way to achieve this was by not letting cottages when they became vacant. Another was to sell off outlying parts of the estate, such as Flaxman's Farm, which he sold in 1963. One wonders, though, why he simply did not sell the whole estate if it was such a burden to him.

Sir Charles Mott-Radclyffe told *The Sunday Times* in 1971 that Ronald was 'actively opposed to modernisation'[196]. He refused to allow electricity cables to cross the estate and the church was lit by gas lamps until 1978. In the early 1960s Ronald had written to Rosa Finch informing her that if she wanted mains water at Rose Cottage she and her husband would have to pay for the connection themselves. Ronald also made her agree in writing that she would stop getting water from 'my' well across the road at Glebe Cottage.

~

Bill Wright was one of about half a dozen children who grew up in the village in the 1950s. They walked to the school in Gresham just as children had done in their parents' and grandparents' time – although by now the roads had been metalled, which made them less muddy in the winter. Bill's parents, Jack and Gladys, lived in the council house nearest the church. Gladys was a district nurse and the N.H.S. required her to have her own transport. She was therefore the second person in the village to own a motor car, more than forty years after Denham purchased his first vehicle. Jack was the foreman at Manor House Farm – where his father Horace had been succeeded first by the Whites, then by the

Denises and more recently by the Wrightons – and also lent a hand to his brother Granville at The Den.

Bill would sometimes help with spring cleaning at the Manor House and wander around while he was there. He remembers rapiers hanging on the wall in the master bedroom and a wonderful music box in a glass case that had keys in the shape of bees and other insects. There were also huge mantraps in the loft that were once used to catch poachers. Catching and prosecuting poachers was certainly not a priority for Ronald Hitchcock and the decline of professional gamekeeping on small estates over the course of the twentieth century meant that pheasants and other game birds were now more prolific in the wild than they once were. Shooting parties would still take place, though, and Bill's father would be given a brace of pheasants to thank him for organising the beaters. Bill remembers a varied, wholesome diet, with duck, turkey or goose from a cousin's farm being served up. There was plenty of fresh fruit too, including gooseberries, strawberries, raspberries, blackberries from the hedgerows, scrumped apples from Denham's orchard, and russet apples from his Aunt Hilda's trees as The Den.

The grounds of the Manor House were no longer immaculate, although Maurice Wiseman and Fred Hudson worked hard to keep them tidy. Ronald asked them to plough up the lawn and plant raspberries. These and other fruits and vegetables were sold to local shops. If a shopkeeper wanted something urgently Maurice would get up early in the morning to prepare it and often worked late into the evening. He never claimed overtime and only his family knew how much he really worked. His wife Ruby and his daughter Rosie lent a hand with the raspberry picking and potato harvesting, and at other busy times. Maurice also kept an eye on the Manor House, especially after there had been some night-time break-ins in the 1960s.

~

Ronald Hitchcock died in May 1970 and left instructions for the Bessingham estate to be sold. What his great-great-grandfather had purchased in 1766 in the days of cheap labour and low taxation had become a heavy burden in the twentieth century. Despite Sheridan Hughes's pleas to be allowed to run the estate, the executors of his grandfather's will went ahead and sold it. Ronald's personal estate was valued at about £120,000, of which £23,000 was paid in estate duty. He gave his trusted and long-serving employee Maurice Wiseman the house he had lived in for many years. The rest of the Bessingham estate was sold and the proceeds held in trust for Ronald's family.

Despite his indifferent attitude to the village and his assertion that he hated going there, it was nevertheless in Bessingham that his ashes were scattered on 22 August 1970, according to his wishes. Perhaps he felt he could be at peace with the village more easily after death and at one with the land of his ancestors. The strong pull of family, and of history, is difficult to resist.

Chapter 14

RECIPE FOR REJUVENATION

In October 1970 *Country Life* carried an advertisement for the sale of a 'residential and sporting estate' that was 'quietly situated' and considered 'ideal for investment'[197]. It contained a total of 555 acres, which was divided into four separate farms and the Manor House, with its gardens and parkland. The farms were Manor House Farm (266 acres), Common Farm (117 ½ acres, which had been farmed by Grantham and Dora Rounce in the 1960s), Den Farm (76 ¾ acres) and Lime Kiln Farm (5 ¾ acres). The Manor House came with 77 ¾ acres 'in hand'. There were also outbuildings, a vacant public house, fourteen vacant cottages and eight occupied cottages. The whole estate was to be sold by auction in the spring of 1971 unless a buyer was found beforehand.

The following April *The Sunday Times* described the condition that Bessingham was in as it faced a future outside the estate environment it had known for centuries:

> The air of neglect grows as you reach the village. Barbed wire and a strong padlock bar the gateway to the empty manor house; the pub is deserted, its windows

broken, a metal pole sticks out forlornly from the wall but no sign swings. The village shop has disappeared and more than half of Bessingham's cottages stand empty and dilapidated[198].

Richard Boyce, who lived near Newmarket, was revealed in the article to be interested in buying the estate. John Shrive, who acted as his agent, sought to reassure tenants who were worried about eviction. I met John twice at his office in Holt before his death in 2014. He told me that the farm workers were anxious about their jobs and their homes, but he did his best to dispel their fears, reassuring them that their security of tenure was guaranteed by law. He had been instructed to sell off the estate in various parcels and offered the tenants the opportunity to stay (and have repairs done to their cottages) or go (and receive compensation). John said that he would have liked to turn the large field to the north of the Manor House into a village green to provide a focal point for the village as at Aldborough, but Sustead parish council rejected the idea.

John Neill of Thurgarton Hall purchased land in the south-east of the estate. Gordon Wrighton bought Manor House Farm and moved his tractors and farm machinery from Northamptonshire. Farming was increasingly mechanised, although it is incredible now to think that as late as the early 1960s horses were still working the land in Bessingham. As machines replaced people, the connection with the land became less intimate. Field names were forgotten and hedgerows and farm tracks were ploughed under to create larger fields that could accommodate the tractors and combine harvesters.

Gordon Wrighton's new combine harvester (top) at Manor House Farm in the mid-1970s. Gordon Wrighton and Jack Wright (bottom) in front of a haystack. Just over a decade earlier Jack's brother Granville was using two horses to work the land at The Den.

The cottages were revamped and sold, and by 1976 the *Eastern Daily Press* reported that the population had doubled in the space of six years, with residents now including 'an international banker, a former chairman of the Greater London Council, an artist and a writer'[199]. Some feared that Bessingham would end up with too many second homes and holiday cottages, but the newspaper declared that the village was 'preserving its identity as a friendly and close-knit community. Fears that it might turn into a collection of holiday cottages have proved unfounded'. They called it a 'recipe for rejuvenation'[200].

Myrtle Abigail, John Tuck's daughter, with some of the younger residents of Bessingham in the 1970s.

In 1976 Maurice Wiseman was diagnosed with cancer and died at the age of 69. Since the estate was sold he had worked part-time for the Denises, who had moved to a small farm elsewhere. His daughter Rosie received a 'very touching'[201] letter of condolence from Ronald Hitchcock's daughter when Maurice passed away. Rosie moved to Aylsham in 1979, her childhood home still being without mains water.

~

According to John Shrive, 'the condition of the estate was one of appalling neglect' in 1971[202]. This was also true of the Manor House itself, which, having reached its 100th birthday, was in serious need of refurbishment. The conservatory had already collapsed and urgent work was needed to the skylight above the hall. Bob and Mary Gamble, who had lived at Manor Farm since 1959, approached John Shrive with an offer to buy the Manor House, claiming they had sufficient funds for its upkeep. John told me that he regretted taking them at their word. It is possible that they regretted the move too. Gerald Butler, who got to know Bob and Mary after purchasing the old coach house and stables in the 1980s and converting them into a house, told me that they tried unsuccessfully to move back to Manor Farm. Bob was known to be tight with his money. He kept the church finances in good order when he served as treasurer but he was extremely frugal with his own money. It is possible therefore that he and Mary did have the funds to pay for the upkeep of the Manor House but were unwilling to spend the money. When builders were hired to repair the skylight they stripped the lead from the roof and water began to seep in, causing irreparable damage.

Bob and Mary were considered eccentrics by the rest of the village and had minimal dealings with their neighbours. They both had interesting backgrounds. Mary had trained at Leeds College of Art, where Henry Moore was one of her fellow pupils, and was also an accomplished musician. It was while working as an art teacher that she met Bob, one of her students. Bob later joined the R.A.F. and had a brilliant career as a fighter pilot, being stationed in the Middle East for several years. Mary painted under her maiden name Mary l'Anson (no relation of the Ansons who once owned Bessingham, as far as I can tell). Her paintings were predominantly of religious scenes and she offered one of her works to the Vatican. She also presented oil paintings of the Stations of the Cross to Calthorpe church, where they still hang on the walls today. When Rosie Wiseman went up to the Manor House one year to sell Remembrance Day poppies, Mary answered the door and told Rosie she would like to paint her as a gypsy. This did not happen, but she did paint Albert Finch and the portrait still remains with his family.

Bob and Mary kept various animals that often looked underfed. At various times they had horses, cattle, sheep and goats, some of which were staked on the grass verges to graze. After several complaints Bob and Mary were banned from keeping animals. Eventually Bob decided to sell off most of the old parkland since he no longer had need for it.

In 2004, on my first visit to North Norfolk after taking an interest in family history, I stayed with my cousins Richard and Inge Spurrell at Thurgarton House. One day Inge cycled around the area with me, showing me the gravestones of various ancestors in local churchyards.

We decided to cycle up the driveway to the Manor House to see if anyone was home, but there was no answer when we called out. I remember the dark, overgrown driveway, the sounds of the geese in the woods, and the fact that the house was completely hidden behind vines and undergrowth despite being just a few feet from us. On another trip four years later I was cycling back to Thurgarton from Bessingham church and decided to take another look on my own. Leaving my bike on the side of the road, I nervously walked along the gloomy driveway. In the intervening years I had heard that Bob Gamble, now a widower, had moved out of the Manor House and into a caravan after the floors began to collapse. He ran a bath on the first floor one day, stepped into it, and ended up on the ground floor. As I was walking along the driveway I noticed a path leading off to the left through the tall grass and weeds. Curiosity got the better of me and I decided to see where it went. I spotted the caravan but thought I should probably head back. Turning around, I saw an old man with a long white beard, bent over and shuffling along, entering the path at the far end. I hesitated for a moment – should I try to hide or should I say something? – but decided to call out and explained who I was and why I was nosing around this gentleman's property.

What followed was a very nice conversation with a charming and pleasant man. Bob spoke of his time at the Manor House and his failing health. He also spoke fondly of Mary, and although she had been gone for seventeen years, she was clearly still very present in his life. He was very much in love with her and little else mattered. He seemed almost oblivious to the fact that around us weeds, vines and trees had taken over his home.

A year after this chance encounter I discovered that Bob's family in Yorkshire had decided that he should move closer to them. The Manor House was put up for auction.

~

My father Julian, a chartered surveyor, attended the auction on 10 September 2009 out of curiosity. Having sat through a seemingly endless number of lots, he was pleased when lot 129 – Bessingham Manor House – finally came around. It was being offered 'with the potential to be returned to its former glory subject to both major capital investment and structural building repairs'[203]. The guide price was in excess of £900,000. The auctioneer immediately came down to £500,000 and the bids that followed got as far as £640,000, which was still below the reserve price.

The following year Norwood Homes made a deal with Bob Gamble's family to purchase the property. They began clearing the undergrowth, discovering the true condition of the house and revealing the wall along the road as well as the remains of the tower. They began making plans to restore the house but their structural engineer's report concluded that it was beyond repair. The district council approved plans for its demolition and the reuse of as many of the original bricks and materials as possible for the construction of a new manor house on a different part of the property. Norwood Homes did not want to start work until a buyer was found, but when they realised this was going to be difficult in the economic climate, they decided to sell.

Along came William and Dawn Hickey, who purchased the Manor House in March 2013 and began a major restoration programme. Windows, doors, floors and roofs were all replaced and after a lot of hard work Bessingham Manor House reopened as self-catering holiday accommodation in 2014. That same year William and Dawn were the very deserved winners of North Norfolk District Council's Graham Allen award for the restoration of an historic property.

~

Although events at the Manor House no longer have an impact on the village as they did between 1766 and 1970, the restoration was very much welcomed by people in Bessingham and seen as a positive sign. The cottages were all looking much better than they did in 1970 and the restoration of the Manor House was the long-awaited final stage of Bessingham's rejuvenation.

I was lucky enough to be in Norfolk in June 2013 when the village held a summer party in the grounds of Rectory Cottage. Newcomers and long-established residents chatted over a glass of wine and looked with genuine interest at a display of old photographs and maps that had been put together. Bessingham has never lost its community spirit, despite the difficult times of the late Victorian agricultural depression and the 'ghost village' years of the twentieth century. It is a village with a unique identity, a deep sense of place and a keen awareness of its own history, and this confidence attracts many non-villagers who come to walk along its footpaths, study its Saxon church tower or paint its landscape. I can only hope that this book does justice to Bessingham's rich heritage and distinct character.

NOTES

1. Cobbett, William, *Political Register* (28 September 1833), quoted in 'Deserters From The Plough,' Alun Howkins, *History Today* (February 1993), p. 32.
2. Rider Haggard, Lilias, *A Norfolk Notebook* (p. 22-23)
3. Bridges, E.M., *Classic Landforms of the North Norfolk Coast* (1991), p. 6.
4. Reid, Clement, *The Geology of the Country around Cromer* (1882), p. 109.
5. Reported in in *Proceedings of the Society of Antiquaries*, Vol. 5 (1870), p. 32-33.
6. Reported in *Archaeological Journal*, Vol. 38 (1881), p. 433-434.
7. literarynorfolk.co.uk, retrieved on 23 August 2016.
8. Phillimore, *Domesday Book: Norfolk* (1984).
9. Rosenthal, Joel, *Margaret Paston's Piety* (2010), p. 113.
10. Blomefield, Francis, *An Essay Towards a Topographical History of the County of Norfolk*, Vol. 8 (1808).
11. Bessingham churchwardens' accounts (1683-1813), Norfolk Record Office, PD 222/15.
12. Ibid.
13. Rye, Walter, *Norfolk Families* (1911).
14. Norfolk Record Society, Vol. 19, *Archdeaconry of Norwich: Inventory of Church Goods temp. Edward III* (1947-1948).
15. Will of William Spurrell of Thurgarton (proved 1664), Norfolk Record Office, ANF 1664, fo. 39, No. 137.
16. Will of William Spurrell of Thurgarton (proved 1807), Norfolk Record Office, ANF 1760-1763, fo. 104.
17. Ibid.
18. Bartell, Edmund, *Cromer, Considered a Watering Place; with Observations on the Picturesque Scenery in its Neighbourhood* (1806), p. 76.

19. Draft letters of William Spurrell in Thurgarton account book (c. 1800-1803), Norfolk Record Office, MC 259/68/2 712 x 4.

20. Ibid.

21. Ibid.

22. Ibid.

23. Will of John Spurrell of Bassingham (proved 1803), Norfolk Record Office, ANF 1802-1804, fo. 173.

24. Letter from James Spurrell to Elizabeth Spurrell (22 April 1805), Norfolk Record Office, MC 259/113 712 x 4.

25. Indenture re. estate of William Spurrell (1808), Norfolk Record Office, MC 259/9/1-2, 696 x 6.

26. Ibid.

27. Memo re. footpath dispute (1816), Norfolk Record Office, MC 259/44, 712 x 4.

28. Collection of letters from Frances Shears to Sarah Spurrell (28 May 1811), Norfolk Record Office, MC 259/114/1-14, 712 x 4.

29. Ibid (6 October 1812).

30. White, William, *History, Gazetteer and Directory of Norfolk, and the City and County of the City of Norwich* (1836), p. 563.

31. Letter from Elizabeth Spurrell to Sarah Spurrell (8 May 1815), Norfolk Record Office, MC 259/115 712 x 4.

32. Sargant, Jane Alice, *A Guide to Cromer and its Neighbourhood, by a Visitor,* 3rd ed. (1855), p. 39-40.

33. Ibid.

34. *The Gardener's Magazine* (1835), p. 701.

35. Clare Read Sewell, quoted in *Reshaping Rural England: A Social History, 1850-1925* by Alun Howkins (1991), p. 15.

36. Daniels, Stephen, *Humphry Repton, Landscape Gardening and the Geography of Georgian England* (1999), p. 69.

37. 'Samuel Johnson' in *Dictionary of National Biography,* Vol. 30 (1892), p. 42.

38. Mathias P., 'The Anchor Brewery' (1953), reprinted in *Brewery History,* special issue 145 (2012), p. 34.

39. Letter from James Spurrell to Elizabeth Spurrell (22 April 1805), Norfolk Record Office, MC 259/113 712 x 4.
40. Ibid.
41. Brewing book, Anchor Brewery (1821), London Metropolitan Archives, ACC/2305/01/531.
42. *The Era* (22 November 1840).
43. *The Norfolk Chronicle* (16 January 1819).
44. 'An Act for Inclosing Lands in the Parish of Bassingham in the County of Norfolk' (1821).
45. Auction details re. sale of Butterfield estate (1837), privately held.
46. Circular re. restoration of Bessingham church enclosed with letter from the Rev. H. C. Fisher to Daniel Spurrell (27 March 1867), on microfilm, Norfolk Record Office, MF/RO 104/2.
47. Letter from William Repton to the Rev. Isaac Avarne (24 September 1804), Norfolk Record Office, AYL 1085.
48. *The Norfolk Chronicle* (22 July 1820).
49. Letter from the Rev. William Walker to William Repton (11 September 1820), Norfolk Record Office, AYL 1085.
50. Letter from William Repton to the Rev. William Walker (23 December 1823), Norfolk Record Office, AYL 1165.
51. Letter from the Rev. William Walker to William Repton (26 December 1823), Norfolk Record Office, AYL 1165.
52. Letter from William Repton to the Rev. William Walker (1 February 1824), Norfolk Record Office, AYL 1165.
53. Ibid.
54. Letter from the Rev. William Walker to William Repton (3 December 1824), Norfolk Record Office, AYL 1165.
55. Ibid.
56. Letter from the Rev. William Walker to William Repton (28 January 1825), Norfolk Record Office, AYL 1165.
57. *The Norfolk Chronicle*, 19 May 1838.
58. Bessingham parish magazine, No. 10 (July 1897).
59. Letter from Daniel Spurrell to Elizabeth Spurrell (15 February, year unknown), privately held.

60. *The London Gazette* (1 July 1842).
61. Letter from Daniel Spurrell to Flaxman Spurrell (1 January 1840), on microfilm, Norfolk Record Office, MF/RO 104/2.
61. Ibid (3 April 1840).
62. Ibid (18 March 1840).
63. Ibid (10 February 1840).
64. Ibid.
65. Ibid (19 January 1841).
66. Sarah Maria Spurrell's death certificate.
67. Letter from Mary Isabelle Spurrell to Charles Henry Spurrell (10 August 1872), privately held.
68. Letter from Mary Isabelle Spurrell to Charles Henry Spurrell (21 August 1872), privately held.
69. Ibid.
70. Letter from Mary Isabelle Spurrell to Charles Henry Spurrell (27 August 1872), privately held.
71. Ibid.
72. Letter from Mary Isabelle Spurrell to Charles Henry Spurrell (4 September 1872), privately held.
73. Ibid.
74. Letter from Mary Isabelle Spurrell to Charles Henry Spurrell (10 August 1872), privately held.
75. Letter from J. M. Barrows to the Rev. Charles Henry Spurrell (undated, early 1890s), privately held.
76. Bessingham labour account book (1878-1879), Norfolk Record Office, NBV 15.
77. Will of Elizabeth Spurrell (proved 1866).
78. Memo written by Sir Samuel Hoare (undated), privately held.
79. *The Norfolk Chronicle* (24 August 1867).
80. Affidavit of Daniel Spurrell (1883), privately held.
81. Circular re. restoration of Bessingham church enclosed with letter from the Rev. H. C. Fisher to Daniel Spurrell (27 March 1867), on microfilm, Norfolk Record Office, MF/RO 104/2.
82. *Eastern Daily Press* (April 1906).

83. Specifications for the restoration of Bessingham church (1869), Norfolk Record Office, PD 222/19.

84. *The Norfolk Chronicle* (27 November 1869).

85. Ibid.

86. Scotland, Nigel, *Methodism and the Revolt of the Field: A Study of the Methodist Contribution to Agricultural Trade Unionism in East Anglia, 1872-96* (1981), p. 241.

87. Letter from Barningham Rectory (probably from the Rev. James Wilson) to Daniel Spurrell (6 September 1872), privately held

88. Kenworthy-Browne, John, *Burke's and Savills Guide to Country Houses, Vol. 3: East Anglia* (1981), p. 89.

89. Messent, Claude, *The Old Cottages and Farm-Houses of Norfolk* (1928), p. 189.

90. Journal of Marion Ives (née Philpott) (1927), privately held.

91. *The Bury and Norwich Post* (21 June 1843).

92. Letter from Daniel Spurrell to Flaxman Spurrell (12 September 1841), on microfilm, Norfolk Record Office, MF/RO 104/2.

93. Bessingham labour account book (1872-1873), Norfolk Record Office, NBV 12.

94. Ibid.

95. Bessingham labour account book (1855), Norfolk Record Office, NBV 8.

96. *The Norfolk News* (15 August 1868).

97. Bessingham labour account book (1874-1875), Norfolk Record Office, NBV 13.

98. Howkins, Alun, *Reshaping Rural England: A Social History, 1850-1925* (1991), p. 15.

99. *The Norfolk News* (23 August 1862).

100. Letter from the Rev. F. E. Arden to the Rt. Rev. Charles Manners-Sutton, Bishop of Norwich (6 January 1825), Norfolk Record Office, DN/NDS 280.

101. White, William, *History, Gazetteer and Directory of Norfolk, and the City and County of the City of Norwich* (1854), p. 391.

102. Margaret Maria Frankland's gravestone, Bessingham churchyard.

103. *The London Gazette*, (14 May 1875).

104. Gresham school board minute books (1897-1903), Norfolk Record Office, C/ED 3/95.

105. Rawcliffe, Carole, *Norwich since 1550* (2004).

106. Certificate issued to William Dewing Spurrell by Charles Turner, master of Pottergate Street Academy, Norwich (1818), privately held.

107. Rider Haggard, Henry, *The Days of my Life*, Vol. 1 (1925).

108. Ipswich School punishment book (1870s), Ipswich School Archives.

109. *The Ipswich Journal* (9 May 1874).

110. *The Ipswich School Magazine* (May 1877).

111. Ibid (April 1877).

112. Blatchly, John, *Paper Exercise for Schoolboys*, in *The East Anglian Daily Times* (2 July 2011).

113. *The Ipswich School Magazine* (November 1876).

114. Ibid (December 1876).

115. Ibid.

116. Ibid.

117. *The Ipswichian* (March 1952).

118. Letter from Martha Douglas Powell to Ipswich School (3 November 1951), Ipswich School Archives.

119. 'SPURRELL, Edmund Denham,' in *Who's Who in Norfolk* (1935).

120. Journal of Denham Spurrell (1889), privately held.

121. *Eastern Daily Press* (January 1952).

122. *City of Norwich: The Report of the Castle Museum Committee to the Town Council* (1914), p. 20.

123. Journal of Denham Spurrell (1889), privately held.

124. Ibid.

125. Rider Haggard, Lilias, *Norfolk Life* (1943), dedication.

126. Journal of Denham Spurrell (1889), privately held.

127. Ibid.

128. Letter from Ted Finch to Jonathan Spurrell (25 March 2010), privately held.

129. Simpson, R. J., *Leaves from my Sketchbook* (1893).

130. *Eastern Daily Press* (April 1906).

131. Ibid.

132. Ibid.

133. *The Journal* (23 April 1976).

134. *The Evening Standard* (16 October 1946).

135. Albert and Rosa Finch's rent book, privately held.

136. *Eastern Daily Press* (October 1949).

137. Ibid.

138. Letter from Rosie Purdy (née Wiseman) to Jonathan Spurrell (6 January 2010), privately held.

139. *Eastern Daily Press* (24 November 1949).

140. *The Norfolk News* (9 July 1870)

141. Letter from Mary Isabelle Spurrell to Charles Henry Spurrell (10 August 1872), privately held.

142. *The Garden* (7 April 1833), p. 304.

143. *The Garden* (30 November 1889), p. 500.

144. Will of Daniel Spurrell (proved 1906).

145. Flaxman C. J. Spurrell's obituary in *Ancient Egypt and the East* (Part II), by W. M. F. Petrie (1915), p. 93-94.

146. *The Gardeners' Chronicle* (26 April 1919), p. 198.

147. Journal of Marion Ives (née Philpott) (1927), privately held.

148. Bulwer-Lytton, Neville (later 3rd Earl of Lytton), *The Press and the General Staff* (1921), p. 30-31.

149. *The Times* (14 August 1929).

150. Memorial to Lt.-Col. Robert John Spurrell in Bessingham church.

151. Minutes of Bessingham parish council and parish meetings (1895-1934), Norfolk Record Office, PC 119.

152. Ibid.

153. Ibid.

154. Published letter from the Rev. E. H. Taylor to the Rev. W. Cass (30 April 1921).

155. Published letter from the Rev. W. Cass to the Rev. E. H. Taylor (3 May 1921), Norfolk Heritage Centre.

156. *The Motor Car Journal*, Vol. 6 (1905).

157. Edwards, George, *From Crow-Scaring to Westminster, An Autobiography* (1922), p. 29.

158, Ibid. p. 67.

159. Emily Mills's election pamphlet (10 December 1894), privately held.

160. Letter from the Rev. H. T. Griffith to Emily Mills (19 December 1894), privately held.

161. Letter from the Samuel Groom to Emily Mills (19 December 1894), privately held.

162. Rejected letter from 'GSL' to *The Daily Press* (1894).

163. Letter from George Edwards to an unknown newspaper (29 January 1895).

164. Letter from George Edwards to an unknown newspaper (1894 or 1895).

165. Letter from the Rev. W. W. Mills to an unknown newspaper (10 April 1896).

166. *The Cromer and North Walsham Post* (22 October 1898).

167. Ibid.

168. *The Cromer and North Walsham Post* (12 November 1898).

169. Ibid.

170. Letter from 'An Exposer' to *The Cromer and North Walsham Post* (14 January 1899).

171. *The Cromer and North Walsham Post* (4 February 1899).

172. Howkins, Alun, *Reshaping Rural England: A Social History, 1850-1925* (1991), p. 144.

173. Note in Bessingham labour account book (1915), Norfolk Record Office, NBV 22.

174. *Eastern Daily Press* (10 September 1897).

175. Howkins, Alun, *Reshaping Rural England: A Social History, 1850-1925* (1991), p. 152.

176. 'Manor Farm, Bessingham,' in the Land Valuation Office survey (1910-1915), The National Archives, IR58 62171-3.

177. *The Dairy World and the British Dairy Farmer* (10 October 1906), p. 152.

178. 'Thurgarton Old Hall, Thurgarton,' in the National Farm Survey records (1941-1943), The National Archives, MAF32 740 512.

179. Information from Alfred Blake to Jonathan Spurrell (2 November 2014), privately held.

180. Ibid.

181. Ibid.

182. Information from Joyce White (née Wright) to Jonathan Spurrell (12 February 2014), privately held.

183. Information from Joyce Knowles (née Mallett) to Jonathan Spurrell (8 February 2014), privately held.

184. Circular re. Bessingham organist fund (March 1919), Norfolk Record Office, OLL 2354/1-3, 322 x 6.

185. Bessingham parish magazine, No. 10 (July 1897).

186. Information from George Finch to Jonathan Spurrell (7 October 2014), privately held.

187. *Daily Mail* (4 April 1966).

188. Ibid.

189. Information from Alfred Blake to Jonathan Spurrell (2 November 2014), privately held.

190. *Eastern Daily Press* (21 December 1963).

191. Ibid.

192. Ibid.

193. Ibid.

194. Ibid.

195. Ibid.

196. *The Sunday Times* (18 April 1971).

197. *Country Life*, Supplement 8 (1 October 1970).

198. *The Sunday Times* (18 April 1971).

199. *Eastern Daily Press* (21 April 1976).

200. Ibid.

201. Letter from Rosie Purdy (née Wiseman) to Jonathan Spurrell (6 January 2010), privately held.

202. Information from John Shrive to Jonathan Spurrell (3 February 2010), privately held.
203. W. H. Brown auction catalogue (10 September 2009).

BIBLIOGRAPHY

Books and papers mentioning the Spurrell family

Blatchly, John, *Ipswich School: A History in Photographs* (2009)

Bulwer-Lytton, Neville (later 3rd Earl of Lytton), *The Press and the General Staff* (1921)

Caiger, Nesta, *F. C. J. Spurrell, Kentish Antiquary and Archaeologist* (1971)

Cox, Horace, *Cox's County Who's Who Series: Norfolk* (1912)

Dew, Walton, *The Monumental Inscriptions in the Hundred of Holt, in the County of Norfolk* (1885)

Fiske, R. C., *The Last Wedding of a Prince of Wales: Bessingham's Salute of 1862* (1981)

Fryer, Alfred, *Fonts with Representations of the Seven Sacraments: Supplement* (1933)

Harvey, J. R., *Records of the Norfolk Yeomanry Cavalry* (1908)

Edwards, George, *From Crow-Scaring to Westminster, An Autobiography* (1922)

L'Estrange, John, *Calendar of Freemen of Norwich from 1317 to 1603* (1888)

L'Estrange, John, *The Eastern Counties Collectanea: Being Notes and Queries on Subjects Relating to the Counties of Norfolk, Suffolk, Essex, and Cambridge* (1872-1873)

Pike, W. T., *Norfolk and Suffolk in East Anglia: Contemporary Biographies* (1911)

Power, D'Arcy, *Plarr's Lives of the Fellows of the Royal College of Surgeons of England*, revised (1930)

Rye, Walter, *Norfolk Families* (1911)

Rye, Walter, *Some Rough Materials for a History of the Hundred of North Erpingham*, 3 vols. (1883-1889)

Sargant, Jane Alice, *A Guide to Cromer and its Neighbourhood, by a Visitor*, 3rd ed. (1855)

Scott, B., and Shaw, A., *The Quiet Man of Kent: The Contribution of F. C. J. Spurrell to the Early Years of Palaeolithic Archaeology* (2009)

Walford, Edward, *The County Families of the United Kingdom* (1913)

Books and papers mentioning Bessingham

Armstrong, M., *Histories and Antiquities of the County of Norfolk*, Vol. 3 (1781)

Blomefield, Francis, *An Essay Towards a Topographical History of the County of Norfolk*, Vol. 8 (1808)

Doubleday, Arthur, *A History of Norfolk*, Vols. 1 and 2 *(1901)*

Faden, William, *Faden's Map of Norfolk* (1797)

Hart, Stephen, *The Round Church Towers of England* (2003)

Kenworthy-Browne, John, *Burke's and Savills Guide to Country Houses, Vol. 3: East Anglia* (1981)

Massingham, R. M., *Where did Granny and Grandad go to School?* (2007)

Mee, Arthur, *The King's England: Norfolk* (1940)

Messent, Claude, *The Old Cottages and Farm-Houses of Norfolk* (1928)

North Norfolk District Council, *Landscape Character Assessment* (2009)

Parkin, Charles, *An Essay Towards a Topographical History of the County of Norfolk*, Vol. 3 (1808)

Pevsner, Nikolaus, *The Buildings of England: North-East Norfolk and Norwich* (1962)

Phillimore, *Domesday Book: Norfolk* (1984)

Reid, Clement, *The Geology of the County around Cromer* (1882)

Rosenthal, Joel, *Margaret Paston's Piety* (2010)

Rye, James, *A Popular Guide to Norfolk Place-Names* (1991)

Scotland, Nigel, *Methodism and the Revolt of the Field: A Study of the Methodist Contribution to Agricultural Trade Unionism in East Anglia, 1872-96* (1981)

Simpson, R. J., *Leaves from My Sketchbook*, Vol. 9 (1893)

Whitaker, William, *The Water Supply from Underground Sources* (1921)

White, William, *History, Gazetteer and Directory of Norfolk, and the City and County of the City of Norwich* (1836-1883)

Other books and papers about Norfolk

Anderson, Verily, *Friends and Relations* (2005)

Anderson, Verily, *The Northrepps Grandchildren* (1968)

Barnes, Pam, *Norfolk Landowners since 1880* (1993)

Bridges, E. M., *Classic Landforms of the North Norfolk Coast* (1991)

Byant, A., *Map of the County of Norfolk* (1826)

Daniels, Stephen, *Humphry Repton, Landscape Gardening and the Geography of Georgian England* (1999)

Entwhistle, Keith, *A Century of Faces and Places: A History of Aldborough and Thurgarton, 1900-2000* (2002)

Ketton-Cremer, R. W., *Felbrigg: The Story of a House* (1962)

le Strange, Richard, *Monasteries of Norfolk* (1972)

Rawcliffe, Carole, *Norwich since 1550* (2004)

Reid, Andy, *Cromer and Sheringham: The Growth of the Holiday Trade, 1877-1914* (1986)

Rider Haggard, Lilias, *A Norfolk Notebook* (1946)

Rider Haggard, Lilias, *Norfolk Life* (1943)

Wade Martins, Susanna, *A History of Norfolk* (1984)

Wade Martins, Susanna, *Changing Agriculture in Georgian and Victorian Norfolk* (2002)

Willins, E. P., *Some of the Old Halls and Manor Houses in the County of Norfolk* (1890)

Other books about history, landscape and society

Hoskins, W. G., *English Landscapes* (1973)

Howkins, Alun, *Reshaping Rural England: A Social History, 1850-1925* (1991)

Howkins, Alun, *The Death of Rural England: A Social History of the Countryside since 1900* (2003)

Nicolson, Adam, *The Gentry: Stories of the English* (2011)

Pryor, Francis, *The Making of the British Landscape* (2010)

Rackham, Oliver, *The History of the Countryside* (1986)

Reader, W. J., *Life in Victorian England* (1964)

Rider Haggard, Henry, *The Days of my Life, Vol. 1* (1925)

Thompson, F. M. L. *English Landed Society in the Nineteenth Century* (1963)

Record offices, archives and libraries

Beinecke Rare Book and Manuscript Library
British Library Newspaper Collection
Gressenhall Farm and Workhouse
Historic England
Ipswich School Archives
National Portrait Gallery
Norfolk Heritage Centre
Norfolk Historic Environment Service
Norfolk Library Service
Norfolk Record Office
Royal Horticultural Society Lindley Library
The National Archives

Newspapers, journals and directories

Archaeological Journal
Baily's Hunting Directory
Brewery History
Country Life
Crockford's Clerical Directory
Daily Mail
Eastern Daily Press
History Today
Kelly's Directories
Norfolk Archaeology
North Norfolk News
Proceedings of the Society of Antiquaries
The Bury and Norwich Post
The Cromer and North Walsham Post
The Evening Standard

The Ipswichian
The Ipswich Journal
The Ipswich School Magazine
The Garden
The Gardeners' Chronicle
The Gardener's Magazine
The London Gazette
The Norfolk Chronicle
The Norfolk News
The Sunday Times
The Times

Websites

bessinghamhistory.org
bessinghammanor.uk
literarynorfolk.co.uk
maps.nls.uk
norfolkmills.co.uk

INDEX

Women are listed under their married names

Abigail, Myrtle (née Tuck),
113, 184
Abigail, Sidney, 113
Aldborough, 3, 18, 74, 88,
107, 163, 182
Amis, Mary, 88
Anson family, 12, 21, 31, 44,
47, 50, 186
Arden, Francis, 91
Armstrong, Skeffington, 74-
75
Avarne, Isaac, 49-50, 67
Aylmerton, 8, 26, 119, 136-
138, 140, 143, 177
Aylsham, 3, 27n, 38n, 49,
69n, 86, 185
Aylsham Navigation, 39
Bacon family, 12, 19, 20n, 23,
51, 87, 150, 156
Baconsthorpe, 5, 121, 123
Barberton, 119, 126
Barclay family, 39-41, 40n,
112, 135, 147, 161
Barclay Perkins & Co., 29,
33, 39-42, 41n
Barningham (or North
Barningham), 3, 8-9, 46, 75,
79, 93, 106-107, 116, 118,
133, 133n, 158
Bayfield family, 66-67

Basa, 6
Batt family, 118, 148, 152
Bear, 108-110
Bessingham Manor House,
3, 12, 22n, 33-34, 39, 41, 55,
60-61, 64-66, 75-80, 82, 83n,
87-88, 90, 98, 103-104, 110,
114, 117-118, 122, 124-125,
133, 137, 147, 150-151, 153,
155-161, 165-166, 172, 179-
182, 185-189
Bessingham parish council
(see Parish council)
Billockby, 66, 68-70, 107, 127,
146
Bishop family, 132, 149-150,
156, 161
Boat Race (Oxford and
Cambridge University), 97
Bond Cabbell, Benjamin, 69,
137
Bond, Mary (née Spurrell),
26-27, 27n
Borrett, John, 133, 164
Boyce, Richard, 182
Blake, Alfred, 158, 175, 177
Blake, Cecil, 150, 153
Boer War, 126
Bowls, 88, 106, 158
Bulwer-Lytton, Neville, 128

209

Thurgarton church, 8, 19, 21, 116, 135
Thurgarton Hall, 19, 20n, 81, 104, 104n, 152, 182
Thurgarton House (or Old Hall), 20, 20n, 22n, 26, 32, 57, 104n, 111, 118, 135, 154, 173, 186
Thwaite, 8, 21, 67, 80
Tuck, Charles John, 134
Tuck Charley, 64-66, 76, 88
Tuck, John, 64-66, 76, 88, 105-106, 111, 113, 117, 134, 146-147, 149, 155-156, 161, 166-167, 184
Tuck, Mary Anne, 134, 155
Turnips, 37, 82-83, 136, 146, 149-150, 152
Walker, William, 50-51
War Agricultural Executive Committee, 153
Watney, James, 43n
White, Joy (née Wright), 154, 158-159, 161, 163, 166
Willcox, Mary (née Ives), 159
Wilson, James, 75, 106
Wilson, Margery ('Margy'), 106-107
Wilson, Mary, 107
Wilson, Thomas Erskine, 121
Windham, William, 48
Wiseman, Maurice, 118, 153, 159, 166, 179-180, 184

Wiseman, Ruby, 118, 153, 159
Wright, Bill, 178-179
Wright, Granville, 151-153, 165-166, 177, 179, 183
Wright, Hilda, 151-153, 165-166, 177, 179
Wright, Horace, 150-151, 153, 161, 165, 178
Wright, Jack, 166, 176, 178, 183
Wrighton, Gordon, 182-183
Yew Tree Cottage, 163-164